Staffordshire Bull Terriers

Dedicated to
the late Laurence G. Rant and the late C.L. 'Boge' Savage

STAFFORDSHIRE BULL TERRIERS

AN OWNER'S COMPANION

V.H. Pounds
and Lilian Rant

The Crowood Press

First published in 1991 by
The Crowood Press Ltd
Ramsbury, Marlborough
Wiltshire SN8 2HR

This impression 1996

British Library Cataloguing-in-Publication Data

Pounds, V.H.
  Staffordshire bull terriers.
  1. Staffordshire bull terrier
  I. Title   II. Rant, Lilian
  636.755

ISBN 1 85223 365 6

Throughout this book, 'he', 'him' and 'his' have been used as
neutral pronouns and refer to both males and females, be they
human or canine.

Line-drawings by Audrey North

Typeset by Taurus Graphics, Abingdon, Oxon

Printed and bound in Great Britain by
WBC Book Manufacturers, Bridgend

Contents

	Preface	6
	Acknowledgements	7
1	The History of the Breed	9
2	The Breed Standard	37
3	Buying your Puppy or Dog	114
4	Care and Management	133
5	Showing and Judging	145
6	Breeding	163
7	Pregnancy and Whelping	176
8	Ailments and Diseases	187
9	Famous Dogs of the Breed	200
10	Living with Staffordshire Bull Terriers	226
	Useful Addresses	235
	Bibliography	237
	Index	238

Preface

Many fine books have been written about the Staffordshire Bull Terrier, and our aim is not to repeat breed history competently covered by others. Rather, we have set out to discover the dog itself and perhaps in so doing will provide a better understanding of this breed by owners, breeders and judges.

We are quite aware of our own shortcomings, preferences and beliefs concerning this breed and expect disagreement with some of our views and findings, but if this book does nothing more than induce genuine interest, study and thought-provoking discussion, we will have achieved our purpose and will, indeed, be well satisfied.

V. H. Pounds (UK)
Lilian Rant (USA)

Acknowledgements

The authors would like to thank the following people. Professor G. Clayton Jones, B.Vet.Med., MRCVS, DVRI, DSAO, University of London, The Royal Veterinary College; Mr G. Swift, MRCVS; Mrs Stephen Dalton (movement photography); Mr Tom Horner; Mrs Thelma Brown; Gabrielle Brentnall and Mrs Jean Williamson, for anatomical plates, based on X-rays and model observation (1982). 'Anatomical plates, no matter how excellent, are essentially two-dimensional; they cannot suggest the full shape of the bones. They can, however, point out proportional relationships and salient areas to be studied. The anatomy of exterior forms can only be guided by the living model. Any interior anatomy must be provided by the corpse, and its dissection or X-rays where skeletal anatomy is being considered, but even these must be supplemented by the living model.'

1

The History of the Breed

The United Kingdom
(V.H. Pounds)

It is known, by virtue of archaeological excavation and by the presence of dogs depicted in the cave dwellings found in the Pyrenees, that man and dog have been companions, albeit through mutual self-interest, for many thousands of years. The history of our canine companions has been explained by many very erudite experts, some of whom have devoted many years of research into this fascinating subject. Our object here, however, is to explore, as far as is possible, the probable history of the breed type now known as the Staffordshire Bull Terrier, and to explain as far as possible why and how both hereditary factors and the environment from which he comes have dictated the type of dog he is today, both physically and mentally.

It was not until after the Norman invasion that the baiting of bulls, bears and badgers, etc. became a popular sport or pastime of the English people. From about the time of Henry II, baiting was an organized spectacle for public entertainment, usually staged near the towns, which leads us to believe they would have been watched, apart from the nobility, by local tradesmen and their apprentices rather than the agricultural workers and serfs. It was probably the growing popularity of these sports that necessitated a division of long-established British fighting dogs into at least two types.

The large and heavy mastiff type was not as fast nor as nimble as smaller variations of the same breed, and over a period of time these rather smaller animals, because of their proficiency, became known as bulldogs. Hundreds of years later, these were again to be reduced in size, when baiting became illegal and dog fighting became the fashion. However, they were not all similar in make or shape to one another: the name would be applied to any dog who was game enough, active and strong enough, to bait and pin a bull, and if

9

needed, to 'throw' it as well. Long-haired or short-haired, fat or thin, if it could do that job it would be defined as a bulldog.

Indeed, in Volume 9 of the *Sporting Magazine* dated March 1822 there is an account of a bull bait held at Durdham Downs near Bristol, in which the successful dog, i.e. the one that eventually pinned the bull, was described as a lanky, dingy red-haired dog, with a head more like a lurcher than a bulldog, and with a short, thick and bushy tail. Make no mistake, this would have been called a bulldog, and a good one too, who would have been used for breeding in the hope that he would pass on his courage and ability. These baiting people were not concerned with conformation, only with effectiveness.

In general, though, the most successful type of dog was more or less as the illustration shown opposite. This is the old bulldog, from which the modern Bulldog, the Bull Terrier, the Staffordshire Bull Terrier and probably many other modern breeds are descended, some containing Bulldog blood to a greater degree than others. I think we may justifiably claim that in both conformation and character, our Staffordshire Bull Terrier now has by far the closest resemblance to this magnificent old breed and is his nearest living relation. Possibly Bulldog breeders will argue that this is not so, but a study of any selection of old Bulldog prints and paintings prior to the middle of the nineteenth century will confirm this opinion.

In the early years of the 19th century, a few enlightened and influential members of the ruling class started to agitate in Parliament for animals to be allowed some rights in law, and in 1809 Lord Erskine, a Scottish lawyer and former Lord Chancellor, attempted to get this principle accepted in Parliament. Eventually, on 22 June 1822, the Bill received Royal Assent. It was a great day indeed for animal welfare.

This bill was of great importance in the history of our breed, as it marked the beginning of the end of many of the cruel sports which had been practised in this country for so many hundreds of years. The popularity of main spectator sports, such as baiting, declined rapidly, but there were many adherents of blood sports who turned to other more easily hidden pastimes to satisfy their desire to be thrilled by watching the indomitable courage of these English dogs. The fighting of dog versus dog and dog versus rats became much more widely practised than hitherto and many dogs became famous champions at these sports.

One of the best known was a dog called Billy, presumably a bull

An old type of bulldog, used both for baiting and fighting.

and terrier cross, who was a much smaller animal than the Bulldog, though of similar type. This dog became famous for his ability to kill rats in a pit at tremendous speed, and it is recorded in the *Sporting Magazine* that on Tuesday, 23 September 1822 he killed 100 rats in under nine minutes. This was for a bet of 20 sovereigns and, according to the report, a crowd of over 2,000 gathered at the Westminster Pit to witness this extraordinary feat of speed and agility. The following year, Billy was able to accomplish this feat in a little over five minutes, and this record, as far as we can ascertain, has never been broken.

For many years this type of sport continued to be practised, but public opinion was gradually turning against them, and in 1824 a meeting was held in London under the chairmanship of Mr Fowell Buxton MP, which founded the Society for the Prevention of Cruelty to Animals. The members gathered evidence of cruelty to any animals, and in its first year the Society was able to bring well over 100 cases to court.

Original bull and terrier cross.

It was during the following years that the predecessors of the breed we know as the Staffordshire Bull Terrier slowly emerged from the crossing of the Bulldog and terriers. There are various opinions about the types of terrier involved, but the Old English Terrier and the English White Terrier seem to be the most generally accepted animals. However, as any dog small enough and brave enough to follow game underground may have been used, the ancestry cannot be determined with any great degree of certainty. All we can be absolutely sure of is that a breed was evolved which was a cross between Bulldogs and terriers, and although black and tan, pied, white or any other colour terrier would be used, this applies equally to the Bulldog.

It must also be noted that there were plenty of true Bulldogs who were so small that the cross of the terrier would have been completely unnecessary. Indeed, with the advent of dog shows in 1860 there were classes (usually well filled) for bulldogs of up to about 20lb (9kg) in weight. The illustration of the Staffordshire Bulldog opposite shows an animal whose size would certainly be no larger than the modern Stafford whom he greatly resembles in conformation. It is known that James Hinks, the 'inventor' of the White Bull Terrier, owned several of these small Bulldogs, and he certainly exported a number of them to France. It is very probable that the French Bulldog evolved from these exports of small English Bulldogs.

There is no doubt at all, however, that the Staffordshire Bull Terrier is the direct descendant of these old Bulldogs and terrier-cross dogs, and has been bred true for far longer than his cousin the Bull Terrier. This is without doubt due to a comparatively small but very devoted section of people who so admired the wonderful qualities of these dogs that they bred them and kept them true, although they were, for a good many years, considered to be and were treated as pariahs, particularly among the show adherents of dog lovers. By far the largest population of Staffords, known variously as pit dogs, bull and terriers (or, as I have heard my father refer to them, cur dogs), lived in various districts of the Black Country, with a few small pockets of supporters to be found in London and some parts of the north of England. The main body of enthusiasts were Black Country men, however, and it is to them that present-day Stafford owners do, and always will, owe a great debt of gratitude.

I have been fortunate enough to have known quite a few of the

Joe Mallen in 1910. Note the strength of the foreface and the straight front of his dog.

founders of the first Staffordshire Bull Terrier Club, founded in 1935. Those I have known were, by and large, most delightful people and great Stafford enthusiasts. They were not demonstrative people, and not all of them were in agreement with those who wanted the breed recognized as a pure breed by the Kennel Club.

The history of the Staffordshire Bull Terrier stock has been written of so many times in earlier publications it really needs no reiteration from us. The bare facts are that the Kennel Club agreed to recognize the Staffordshire as a thoroughbred breed, and ruled that the registration would be allowed, for a fee of ten shillings (50 pence) with one or both parents unregistered. Many of the earliest Staffords were registered in this way and, indeed, Bill Boylan has recorded that he invented the names of both the sire and dam of

*One of S. Stone's early imports from England, Bandits Firestreak
Red Rover, a red dog bred by Lady Bowen Buscarlet.*

his dog Game Lad, one of the breed's earliest big winners, and who, moreover, sired the breed's second dog Champion, Game Laddie. All the earliest registered Staffords were good, typical specimens of the breed, which in itself says volumes for the degree of integrity shown by the early members.

Mr H. N. Beilby, in his book first published in 1943 (revised in 1948), categorized the well-known winning dogs – who were mainly used as the most popular sires of wholly registered stock – into lines for dogs, and families for bitches. For many years this was of great use to conscientious breeders who were trying to obtain a type of Stafford, as it gave a narrower selection of the type to choose from. Unfortunately most breeders, however, seemed largely to disregard the family the bitches came from. This resulted in these lines becoming so interrelated that they are now of little use to breeders. Mr Alf Tittle of Manchester, a very well-known breeder and exhibitor, is the only person in the breed now whom we would consider a great authority in being able to trace the lines of dogs and families of bitches to the present-day exhibition animals. Mr Tittle has devoted years of research to making records of the antecedents of a great many of our present Staffords, and has done work which will, we are sure, be of inestimable worth to any pedigree historian of our breed.

The United States of America
(Lilian Rant)

There can be no argument that the Father of the Breed in the USA is Mr Steve Stone, now an English Professor at the University of Nebraska at Omaha. Steve took his wife and two children to Finland and, having always had a family dog, looked around for a suitable mongrel only to discover Finland had no mongrels. He visited the Finnish Kennel Club to do research and found a copy of *Dog World Annual* from England, within which was a John Gordon's Bandits advertisement with a picture of a Staffordshire Bull Terrier. He decided immediately that he wanted a Staffordshire Bull Terrier and contacted Mr Gordon, ordering a bitch pup to be sent to him in Finland as the Breed's first representative in that country. She arrived on 6 April 1964. Bandits Belle Lettres – Bella to the family – grew to be a smallish but otherwise superb adult bitch.

Through Mr Stone's enthusiasm for the breed, he was asked to import more Staffordshire Bull Terriers and, by May 1966, there were nineteen Staffordshire Bull Terriers living in Finland. Mr Stone was one of the founding members of the Finland's Northern Star Staffordshire Bull Terrier Club, and before long he had also introduced the breed in Sweden.

In late 1965, he stated in the English Magazine *The Stafford* that he intended to return to the United States to found a Staffordshire Bull Terrier Club. Fanciers from England sent the names of the three Stateside families who were known to own the breed, but well-meaning friends said he would be pursuing a fool's errand since the United States already had Bull Terriers, Miniature Bull Terriers, American Staffordshire Terriers and Pitbull Terriers crowding the market. They felt that the Staffordshire Bull Terrier would never be able to acquire a following in the USA. Fortunately, Mr Stone felt they were wrong.

Bill Boylan judging Crufts 1948 – one of the original Staffordshire Bull Terrier breeders.

The Stone family arrived back in the USA in Los Angeles, California in August 1966 and by late December had located virtually every Staffordshire Bull Terrier in the nation. There were seven families owning a total of fourteen Staffordshire Bull Terriers, scattered from New York to Chicago to Los Angeles, all of them keen to organize and work towards eventual American Kennel Club acceptance.

He chose 14 January 1967 as the date of the founding of the breed in the United States of America, headquartered in Pasadena, California. In addition to setting up a Breed Registry, he began advertising modestly, but regularly, in *Dog World* magazine while doing local promotion in the *Los Angeles Times* and local radio pet shows, as well as lots of personal public relations.

Immediately responses and results started coming in. Within weeks, several families wanted puppies and he ordered them from the late Marian Forester in New Zealand and from Colin Smith in the United Kingdom. Most were bitch puppies and it was explicitly understood that they were to be bred from, if of sufficient quality.

17

At that time, as every effort was directed toward increasing breed numbers and strength, neutering or spaying were concepts we did not readily embrace.

By the summer of that year, several domestic litters were registered as owners scattered throughout the country began breeding their stock. Numbers soared mightily, up to nearly a hundred, and the breed began to attract attention both locally and nationally, mostly positive. Once the ranks of Staffordshire Bull Terrier owners began to swell across the nation, Mr Stone decided it was time for the SBTC/USA Club to become a representative organization for the breed. After writing to the six other founding members to poll their opinion, which was unanimously favourable, he called an organized meeting in Los Angeles.

Prior to this, I had been searching for a Staffordshire Bull Terrier pup. I had found American Staffordshire Terriers, Bull Terriers, Miniature Bull Terriers, Pitbull Terriers but no Staffordshire Bull Terriers. Since my husband Larry and I were shortly to be visiting England where I knew I could find the breed, I gave up looking for it in the USA. However, a few weeks before we were due to leave on our trip, Larry told me he knew where there was a red Staffordshire Bull Terrier bitch pup for sale, which information I ignored. I was totally convinced the breed did not exist in the United States of America. Rather unwillingly I agreed to go and view the pup only because an appointment had been made and it would have been less than courteous not to have kept it.

We arrived at the house and the door opened. To my disbelieving eyes, and great joy, there to greet us were two adult Staffordshire Bull Terriers, a dog and a bitch, both red in colour and each wearing the usual Staffordshire Bull Terrier welcoming grin. They were Firestreak Red Rover who became a very special friend of mine, and his mate Bandits Belle Lettres. Tucked away in a corner of the room, fast asleep, was their offspring, a lovely little red bitch pup, and I knew I had found my beloved 'Charliegirl' – Bearcats Bellamore. Her registration number in the Club Stud Book kept by Mr Stone was No. 23 and, of course, we became members of the Club.

Maini and Steve agreed to house Charliegirl during our scheduled visit to England. When there, we paid a visit to John Gordon who showed us a red male pup that was for sale and, of course, we bought him. He was Tinkinswood Imperial ('Fred') and was destined to play a major role in the early history of the breed in the United States of America. Fred was entered into the Club's Registry

Ch. Tinkinswood Imperial, another of the first imported English-bred dogs. Exported to Mrs Lilian Rant by Mr J.F. Gordon.

as No. 31 on 20 October 1967, giving us a total of seven Staffordshire Bull Terriers in the State of California. Years later, he was given the honour of being the first Staffordshire Bull Terrier registered with the American Kennel Club, on the proposal of Mr Steve Eltinge and at the request of the Board of Directors of the Staffordshire Bull Terrier Club of America. He became the first Dog Champion of the Breed.

Relentlessly Steve pursued his 'exposure' plan for the breed. He directed us, with our dogs, to sit for hours in various shopping malls, encouraged by the store owners as an attraction to bring in customers; arranged for the breed to participate in the Hollywood Boulevard Dog Parade, which activity, I fear, was not one of our best efforts. We met in local parks, walked our dogs in groups in various areas of Los Angeles and were required to take them whenever possible to wherever we were heading.

Inevitably, there were some unwanted dogs and orphan pups but all were taken care of. A litter of pups found in a pet store on the East coast, sent there from Ireland, was promptly purchased and shipped to Los Angeles. We shared the care of unwanted Staffordshire Bull Terriers and I well remember being the recipient of six unwanted five-week-old pups who arrived at our home at Thanksgiving (November), celebrated Christmas with us and the last pup left the following Easter! More pups and young dogs and bitches were imported, more litters were arriving and more owners joining our ranks.

In 1969 Steve announced he was taking his family to Omaha, Nebraska to pursue his career. We were extremely sorry to see him and Maini leave and I was particularly saddened that Brutus (Firestreak Red Rover) went with them. To me, Brutus was one of the best dogs we had. He was full sized, of superb construction with the required long, athletic resilient muscles and had the correct temperament. Brutus was always in top condition. Steve believed, as I have always believed, and still do, that this breed must be exercised and often we met Maini and Steve with our dogs and spent hours climbing and walking the hills that surround Los Angeles.

When invited by the Midwest fanciers to conduct a workshop on the breed at Omaha, I was able to visit the Stone family and saw Brutus again, a few months before he died. Bella (Bandits Belle Lettres) had died earlier.

I think it correct to say Bandits Belle Lettres and Firestreak Red Rover were the foundation stock of the Breed in the United States. Had both dogs not been advanced in years by the time we were able to compete in the American Kennel Club show ring, they would have been worthy Champions.

As would be expected, with the arrival of the Stone family in the Midwest, Staffordshire Bull Terriers began to appear there. In Maryland, Claude Williams was steadily increasing our numbers, as was Mrs Rosenfield in Massachusetts.

In 1968 the Staffordshire Bull Terrier Club of America emerged in California under President Kenneth Tinckler and later William Daniels. Larry Rant was the Secretary under both Presidents and, after two visits to the American Kennel Club in New York, rewrote the by-laws that would be acceptable for eventual registration of our breed by the AKC and, looking further down the road, acceptance as the Parent Club. Under the Club we had many activities including our own breed matches and discussion sessions on the breed, and we invited, housed and fed overseas judges in return for conducting workshops and judging.

However, the road appeared to be a long one and we began to believe that acceptance of the Breed by the American Kennel Club was, indeed, nothing more than an impossible dream. As often happens, an opportunity suddenly presents itself to further a cause, and one such opportunity came from a telephone call I received. The caller was Gus Bell, an Akita fancier who enquired if we would, as owners of a rare breed, be interested in joining other rare-breed owners – also in quest of recognition as a pure-bred breed by the American Kennel Club – in forming an organization to be called the Association of Rare Breeds of California. Naturally, we were extremely interested and joined the Association.

The Association held its first Fun Match in 1970, receiving an entry of 255 dogs from thirteen different breeds and attended by fanciers from throughout the United States. Fun Matches sponsored by ARBC continued and gradually rare breed organizations appeared throughout the country. Gus Bell was the driving force in the success of the Association and, to our great regret, two years after acceptance of his breed by the American Kennel Club, he died from a heart attack.

Under the Dog Show Rules, a provision for a Miscellaneous Class stretches back to the earliest years of the American Kennel Club, designed for dogs for whom regular classification was not offered at a show and who were eligible for further competition. In 1924, the rule changed, precluding dogs from the Miscellaneous Class from competing in Variety Group Competition. In 1955 the Rules for Registration and Dog Shows for the first time included a list of breeds eligible for the Miscellaneous Class and at that time a policy concerning the admission of new breeds was apparently established.

It is extremely difficult and disappointing to accept that our breed, one of the most popular in England, registered as a pure-bred dog under The Kennel Club on the basis of a Pedigree and found in many countries, was not automatically accepted and admitted to Stud Book registration by the American Kennel Club and that it was first required to compete in the Miscellaneous Class.

There is, however, a sensible reason. A breed might well be popular elsewhere and registered as a pure breed by Kennel Clubs, but will there be sufficient interest in this new breed in the USA? Will it be kept true to type? Is the breed here to stay and flourish or will interest wane and the breed fade from the American dog

21

One of Mrs Rant's early imports, Northwark Silverlake Sal – from Australia this time.

world? There is, though, a 'plus' side for the fancier. This Class provides an opportunity for fanciers to acquire the art of showing a dog, learn the American Kennel Club Rules and Regulations on showing a dog and, most important, gives a new breed much-needed public exposure.

The Miscellaneous Class requires all breeds to be judged together in one class under an ILP (Indefinite Listing Privilege) number, and winning placings are one to four. There can, therefore, be a winning line-up of four different breeds. The first placed dog is not eligible to compete in Group competition.

The Staffordshire Bull Terrier was admitted into this class as of January 1972 and we entered the breed in the prestigious Beverly Hills Kennel Club Show at Los Angeles, where to our satisfaction we won our first AKC ribbon by virtue of the fourth placing of Tinkinswood Imperial. Naturally, we celebrated. Over the years I have been fortunate enough to win many more ribbons but I must confess the only one I have kept was the first.

We were quite comfortable in the Miscellaneous Class and knew many of the exhibitors whose breeds were members of the Association of Rare Breeds of California. Competition was keen but friendly. We had good judging and poor judging, the latter evidenced when we were told to move our Maltese Terriers to the other side of the ring. Spectators were interested and asked us about our breed, referring to them as anything from strange, ugly and weird, to handsome, cute and likeable.

The owners of the Miscellaneous Class breeds tended to stay together and we spent most of our time discussing and scheming how to move the American Kennel Club to accept our breeds into the Stud Book, knowing full well that American Kennel Club was unmovable. It was a time of excitement and frustration. We knew we had to keep the entries as high as possible and, caravan style, we travelled hundreds of miles to enter as many AKC Shows as possible to ensure healthy entries.

Prifddinas Petrina, a good bitch imported from Wales before Staffordshire Bull Terriers were recognized by the American Kennel Club.

In November 1972 we were pleased and envious when the Akita left the Miscellaneous Class and were well aware their sojourn there was for seventeen years (1955–72). The Bichon Frises were also moving out of the Class; we did not regret this, having found that breed to be the hardest to beat.

In 1974 the wonderful day arrived when I found a letter in our mailbox from the American Kennel Club advising us that, as of 1 October 1974, two years after entry into the Miscellaneous Class, our breed was eligible for registration and entry into the Stud Book. There would be much work to do, the most important being the research and proving of pedigrees.

Finally, the three people who were the principal players in reaching our goal must be recorded: Steve Stone, who through his enthusiasm and hard work founded the Breed in the United States; Larry Rant, who, as the Club Secretary, reorganized the first Breed Club and produced by-laws conforming to the requirements of the American Kennel Club for registration of the breed and the future event of Parent Club; and C.L. Savage, who had such a kindly interest in our breed, gave us wise counsel and smoothed the rocky path to our goal.

The Purpose of the Breed

Most, if not all, of existing breeds of dog have been obtained either by what is known as selective breeding, i.e. breeding for certain purposes, from types of dog whose physical construction and instinct are most nearly suitable for the purpose. Also, full and effective use has been made of mutations where a genetic abnormality has occurred in which the progeny have differed entirely from the physical conformation of both sire and dam, and from what they would be expected to produce.

Before dog shows became fashionable, practically all dogs were bred for some particular purpose and a dog which was no use for the purpose for which he was bred was either disposed of or very occasionally kept as a pet, but in any event would never be used for breeding. Only animals which measured up to the requirements of the purpose were used as breeding stock and generally only the very best were used to any extent. Naturally, this process gradually improves the general qualities of the animal's ability in its specialized field. With the advent of dog shows, which after all are

Ch. Piltdown Bill of Truestaff. Bred by V.H. Pounds and owned by L. Rant.

really canine beauty exhibitions, the Standards of particular types of dog were formed from what, at the beginning, were the most successful dogs of any type for the purpose for which they were bred.

This was, and is, all very well, but over a period of time, and usually after that purpose is no longer of prime importance to its survival, a general smoothing out of controversial physical points is apparent and called for in a breed. This is largely influenced by a few specimens who are exhibited in the show ring with great success and whose physical make-up is considered to be ideal for the original purpose, but whether this is really so can only ever be a matter of opinion, since the dog is no longer being used for his original purpose.

To understand any breed of dog, particularly from the point of view of the serious breeder and judge using the Breed Standard, there must be some fairly clear knowledge of that breed's original

25

purpose. What then was the original purpose for the Staffordshire Bull Terrier?

This breed is a comparative newcomer to the show ring although its lineage is believed to be extremely long, stretching back into the past to the Roman Conquest of Britain. Recognition and entry into the Stud Book of The Kennel Club in England came in 1935 and in The American Kennel Club in 1975.

The name of the breed suggests a cross between the Bulldog and terrier, but this must not be considered a cross between the present-day Bulldog and terrier. From old drawings, the structure of the present-day Staffordshire Bull Terrier appears to resemble more closely the early Bulldog.

There are many theories of the original purpose for this breed, some from early books, stories handed down from one generation of owners to another, and all seemingly shrouded in a degree of misinformation, lack of knowledge, wishful thinking based on personal preference of origin, and often downright myth. In recent years, there has been an unshakeable belief that this breed evolved solely as a pit-fighting animal and it may well have been so used for a short period of time. However, due consideration must be given to the extent of influence gained from the bull-baiting ancestry known to exist in this breed.

The Staffordshire Bull Terrier, particularly when encouraged or forced, will put up a fight (as will most other breeds). When thus engaged, he invariably proves his inheritance from his great Bulldog ancestry of enormous courage and tenacity, often to his own disadvantage since we believe that the present-day construction is not that of a truly proficient fighting dog. In this regard, though, we are quite sure that two dogs of any breed, if willing, are just as capable of putting up a fair performance. Surely it can hardly be suggested that two dogs of any breed fighting each other proves that they were bred for fighting and that was, therefore, their original purpose?

The only breed, we believe, that can honestly be regarded as an efficient dog-fighting animal, scrupulously bred for that purpose by dedicated breeders devoted to that sport (even in this day of supposed enlightenment), is the American Pitbull Terrier. The conformation of the APBT has been altered considerably from that of his Staffordshire Bull Terrier ancestry following the breeders' quest for greater efficiency for its task. Since our exploration of the origin and purpose of the Staffordshire Bull Terrier appears to us to lie between pit-fighting and bull-baiting, we are confining ourselves to comparison of the Staffordshire Bull Terrier with the American Pitbull Terrier, as the latter is acknowledged as a truly superb example, by its conformation, of a dog-fighting animal. Regrettably, some are still used for this purpose, albeit illegally.

The American Kennel Club opened its Stud Book to the American Pitbull Terrier in the 1930s as the 'Staffordshire Terrier', later to be called 'American Staffordshire Terrier' when the Staffordshire Bull Terrier gained recognition in the USA in 1975. Therefore, today we have three breeds – the Staffordshire Bull Terrier, the American Staffordshire Terrier and the American Pitbull Terrier – all acknowledged to emanate from an original cross of the Bulldog and terrier, but now showing definite differences in type and structure, although sharing similarity in the Breed Standards.

The other members of this family, the Coloured and White Bull Terrier, are also acknowledged to be of direct descent from the Bulldog and terrier cross. The Bull Terrier has had a distinct advantage in that it was, to a great degree, conceived by one family (Hinks) who dedicated themselves to refining the breed and laying a sound basis for generations to come. Today's fanciers are clearly retaining type.

It would be a grave mistake if we did not make it clear, from our own extensive knowledge of American Pitbull Terriers, that they are not all used for dog-fighting, though the physical capability is retained. Indeed, under the guidance of The United Kennel Club in Kalamazoo, Michigan, USA there are now many Championship Conformation Shows available to exhibitors under a Breed Standard, resulting in the showing of superb animals both in conformation and temperament. We are well aware that there is unwarranted prejudice against this breed, particularly in the United Kingdom, due to misinformation and lack of knowledge of the existence of a non-fighting pure-bred American Pitbull Terrier. At this stage in their evolution as a show dog, and not a fighting dog, they must bear the same stigma of cur or fighting dog that the Staffordshire Bull Terrier and the American Staffordshire Terrier had to endure during their emergence as show dogs. We understand the Staffordshire Bull Terrier had great difficulty in obtaining recognition by The Kennel Club as a pure-bred dog because it was considered to be an undesirable member of the domestic canine family. The Bulldog, so much admired and respected today, was also regarded as an undesirable animal of unsavoury character.

We consider that show specimens of the American Pitbull Terrier are some of the most magnificent dogs it has been our good fortune to know. The United Kennel Club makes it clear that registration is not available for any American Pitbull Terrier known, or suspected, to be used in the pit. Under UKC and well-run Breed Clubs, owners and exhibitors are determined and succeeding in proving the worth of this fine dog as a dog, not a fighting dog.

If the forebears of the Staffordshire Bull Terrier were used extensively for one specific purpose, that of bull-baiting, for a long period of time, this would show in the breed's basic structure, even though that original purpose had a short period of change to pit-fighting. The present-day Staffordshire Bull Terrier Standard and live specimen, we consider, does not reveal a pit-fighting dog. Neither does it reflect the amount and effect of the terrier influence. We must then set out to discover, if we can, the original purpose of this breed and its relationship with the present-day Breed Standard.

Origin and purpose, if known, should be fully described in the Breed Standard. The Standard, at best, is a very brief guide to the desired construction of the dog. Being aware of the origin and purpose of the breed makes the Standard workable and more easily interpreted. If there is no stated origin and purpose, the Standard is open to misinterpretation unless, as is attempted in this book, the dog is studied as well as is possible through proven anatomical construction and attention to historical facts to discover whether the Standard produced the dog or the dog produced the Standard.

Standards are directives of the construction of the breed and reflect the activity it was expected to perform, even if it is not now required for this activity. The name of the dog should give some indication of the origin and purpose. The name of our breed, therefore, gives us the information that it was conceived in or restricted to Staffordshire from a cross of the Bulldog and terrier. Today's Bulldog competes in the Non-Sporting Group in the USA, Utility in the UK, and all terriers appear in the Terrier Group. By the name of this breed, we should either be in the Non-Sporting, the Utility Group or the Terrier Group. We compete in the Terrier Group and, over the years, it is a fact that the Staffordshire Bull Terrier is very seldom given a Group win or placement. Does this lack of high ring honours lie with the exhibits, Breed Standard, judges or the Group in which we are competing?

In the UK the breed is judged almost exclusively by a specialist judge who is, or has been, a breeder/exhibitor. This is not the situation in the USA where the breed is almost exclusively judged by terrier judges. The responsibility for selecting the specimen to represent the breed in the Group lies with the Breed judge, and for placing in the Group both that judge and the All-Terrier Group judge must agree on the excellence of the dog. Statistics show they very seldom do. Are there then diverse opinions between the Breed and Group judges of what constitutes a worthy specimen, or is it the fault of the exhibit? Obviously, there may have been poor specimens selected as Best of Breed and sent into the Group ring, but we believe this would be an exception rather than the rule.

Does the fault lie with the Breed Standard? We do not think so. Rather we are of the opinion the answer lies largely in the word and classification of 'terrier'. Is the Staffordshire Bull Terrier a terrier? Should he compete in the Terrier Group?

Over the years, good breeders have consistently tried and generally have been successful in breeding dogs to fit the Standard, the Bible of the Breed. This then leaves us with two questions. Is our Standard that of a terrier and if so can it be that generations of breeders throughout the world, without consultation with each other, consistently seriously misinterpret the directives of that Standard? Such a thesis is in no way supportable.

What is a terrier? From *The Concise Oxford Dictionary* it is thus:

Small, active handy dog able to pursue fox, etc. into earth.

This description of size does not fit the larger terriers such as Airedale, Kerry Blue or Irish Terrier and, after our recent experience of having to rescue the family Bull Terrier, who, when trying to follow her companion Jack Russell Terrier into a foxhole, became thoroughly stuck, we cannot totally accept the definition that all terriers pursue into the burrow. We can, however, attest to the very good humour of the Bull Terrier during this hilarious operation.

Can we establish from historical facts from old books, if facts they are, the true origin and purpose of our breed? Capt. L. Fitz-Barnard in *Fighting Sports* (1928) wrote:

The original bull-and-terrier had, roughly, a bull-dog's head on a terrier body but his head was rather longer than the bull-dog; still he was a short-faced dog.

He further mentions:

The terrier was not known, but it was probably the old English Terrier, a white dog and I believe the breed is now extinct.

Fitz-Barnard continued in his chapter on fighting dogs:

You will notice I speak of fighting-dogs and not bull-terriers, the reason is that, as I have said before, the showman has appropriated this name. The show bull-terrier was bred from the Bull-and-terrier or fighting-dog, and it is a fine example of what breeding by selection can do. From a chubby-faced dog of all colours they have produced an animal with a face a yard long, and practically always pure white, but they have lost the courage.

Could this description be that of the Bull Terrier since his writing was 1928 after the admission of the Bull Terrier to The Kennel Club Stud Book? We presume the terrier he describes as the old English Terrier, a white dog, was described under English Terrier by Meyrick in *House & Sporting Dogs* (1861):

There are two varieties of this dog [the English Terrier] – one used as a toy dog and bred with a view to his ornamental points; the other, a heavier strong and gamer dog, which has probably at some period received a cross of the Bull-dog.

Meyrick reports that the Old English White Terrier weighed an average of 8lb (3.5kg), and toy dogs 3 to 4lb (1 to 2kg). He continues with The Bull Terrier:

It is current axiom among dog fanciers that no gameness can be got in any dog without a taint or cross of the Bulldog. The bull-terrier is a signal proof of this theory; for the pure Terrier, though active, is by no means distinguished for pluck; whereas the bull-terrier is scarcely inferior in this quality to the Bulldog himself, and in vivacity and activity he surpasses him. The bull-terrier varies greatly according to the predominance of either terrier or the Bulldog blood. It is difficult, however, to decide from the appearance of the dog how much he owes to each breed. As a rule, when the nose is short and the jaw much underhung the Bulldog predominates, but this is not invariable. There are certain marks by which the bull-terrier may always be distinguished; namely, a great breadth of jowl, which gives enormous power to the grip, depth in the brisket and chest; a peculiar roundness to the stifle-joint accompanied by a well let down hock but the most characteristic and unmistakeable point is the small eye which becomes round the moment that the dog's attention is excited. The pure terrier's eye always remains long and narrow. The bull-terrier, in addition to these points, should have straight legs and strong well-developed hind quarters.

With the exception of the small eye, this could easily be related to the present Standard's description of the Staffordshire Bull Terrier.

A great deal was written on these breeds by Idstone in *The Dog* (1872):

The Bulldog – of his origin there are few records; but undoubtedly he has existed for many centuries and has been looked upon as the typical dog of England. Jesse states that the first mention of the Bulldog occurs in a letter written by Prestwich Eaton, from St Sebastian, to George Wellingham in St Swithin's Lane, London in 1631 or 1632 for a good Mastiff, a case of bottles replenished with the best liquor and two good 'bulldogs'.

About the year 1840 very few thoroughbred examples existed and the possession of such an animal would have been regarded as a sure sign of ruffianism. They were to be obtained in London and Birmingham, the latter place and the 'black country' having a kindly feeling towards them. They were white with a patch of brindle on the eye; leggy and with the 'rose ear'. One of the first Bulldogs exhibited, which was worthy of the name, belonged to Mr James Hinks of Birmingham.

The true Bull Terrier, that is a dog with more than one fourth Bull, or the fourth cross, shows no Bulldog ancestry in the casual observer, though it is clearly defined to a judge's eye. Of course, he may be half Bull; beyond that infusion he degenerates into a mongrel Bulldog.

The intelligence of the Bull Terrier is most remarkable. Indeed, the sense of crossed breeds is quite equal, and I think, superior to that of the highest-bred ones; but it must be remembered that such extra care is taken of prize-winners that they lead an artificial life. Prize Setters, Deerhounds, Fox Terriers or Field Spaniels rust away their lives; they are too precious to be risked in their vocation! The mongrel, such as the Lurcher, or Bull Terrier or the cheap Sheep Dog, not considered worth the expense of a collar and chain, is man's constant helper and companion, and shares in, rivals or excels him in intelligence.

In the books we have read, there are differences in the description of the Bull Terrier. Fitz-Barnard gave two different descriptions: one fitting the Bull Terrier, while the other could well be interpreted as the Staffordshire Bull Terrier. However, this book was written in 1928 when the Bull Terrier was already established in the show ring and the Kennel Club Stud Register.

Our conclusion is that a 'bull and terrier' dog was conceived to be used for the pit after, and probably to replace, the outlawed sport of bull-baiting. We must also conclude the cross developed into two types of bull-terrier that are the direct forebears of the present-day Bull Terrier and the Staffordshire Bull Terrier, giving clear differences in type, the first perhaps showing more terrier influence than Bulldog and the latter more Bulldog influence than terrier.

There can be no doubt in our minds that they are, in fact, related breeds. Why then did they develop separately? We think the answer lies simply with social status and geographic location. In Victorian Britain, rigid class distinction was observed. Every man had his social level and the division was one of birth. We conclude that it became the prerogative of the ruling class to own the Bull Terrier while the Staffordshire Bull Terrier became primarily the breed of the working class – the coal miners, ironworkers, labourers, etc.

In that era there was an excellent rail network, providing train transportation through the country if the price of a ticket was within the budget of the user and if there was a station within reach of the area in which one resided. Other than rail travel and except within city limits, there was little public transportation. Obviously then, there was very localized social interaction without benefit of significant outside communication. The construction and type of dog would have varied, often quite considerably, from one area to another.

Prior to 1935, when recognition was granted by The Kennel Club, the dog now known as the Staffordshire Bull Terrier had neither name nor pedigree other than word of mouth assurance that the offspring was sired by 'Joe Bloggs's Jim' and the dam was 'my bitch Rosie'. This, certainly, was a very unreliable method of producing any semblance of stability or similarity, although many physical characteristics were shared by the more typical specimens.

A Standard had to be written and the authors had to bear in mind this variation in breed type. The late Mr H.N. Beilby, one of the most active and erudite members of this group of enthusiasts, has recorded that the Standard was the subject of long and careful discussion. The knowledge and accumulated experiences of fanciers of this dog were discussed, together with available records and photographs. Agreement was reached and the unanimity was surprising, indicating that those breeders had a clear mental picture of the ideal Staffordshire Bull Terrier.

Mr John F. Gordon, undoubtedly the breed's most noted historian, asserts that Shaw's Jim, later named Jim the Dandy, and Pegg's Joe, later named Fearless Joe, were two males considered to be typical, and the 1935 Standard was guided by their construction. There is no evidence that any part of the Standard gave consideration to the construction of an ideal bitch.

Although this was a newly recognized breed by The Kennel Club it had a long history as a type of dog but with variation in size and conformation. To give opportunity and encouragement to exhibitors to compete with some prospect of success in the show ring, the Standard was intentionally written as loosely as possible and to guide breeders to the considered ideal.

There is little doubt that some, but by no means all, of the original show Staffordshire Bull Terriers indicated terrier ancestry through physical features and temperament, although how much and by what terrier can only ever be a matter of conjecture. It is, however, significant that winning animals were generally those in type and physique toward Bull rather than terrier influence.

The Standard was in use from its inception in 1935 until the replacement in 1948, a period of 13 years. However, for six of those years Britain was at war (1939–45) and little showing or breeding was possible, more so in that there was a travel restriction of 25 miles. This gave little or no opportunity for comparison of specimens from different areas, coupled with the fact the majority of enthusiasts were temporarily unable to pursue canine-related interests.

The 1935 Standard was short-lived, effective for a period of six years; four years from 1935–39 and two years from 1946–48. In 1948, it was agreed that a new or revised Standard was necessary to produce a more clearly defined directive. A Meeting of Club Representatives was convened in Wolverhampton. The numbers of delegates from the existing Clubs were:

Staffordshire Bull Terrier Club.	4 delegates
Southern Counties Staffordshire Bull Terrier Society.	4 delegates
North West Staffordshire Bull Terrier Club.	4 delegates
Northern Counties Staffordshire Bull Terrier Club.	1 delegate
Scottish Staffordshire Bull Terrier Club.	4 delegates

Of these 17 delegates, 8 were members of the Parent Club.

Decisions made at that meeting were by a simple majority and Mr Nap Cairns, one of the Southern Counties Staffordshire Bull Terrier Society delegates has stated there was no evidence of any Club having held a prior Meeting for members to discuss the proposed changes in the Standard. It seems that the rank and file of the Staffordshire Bull Terrier fraternity were not consulted.

The changes, accepted by The Kennel Club, were superficial, with one exception which was to change the breed considerably, create argument, even bitterness and anger from the Club Members who, rightly it seems, felt the change was forced upon them with no consideration of their views or their majority approval. The change was the reduction in height from 15in to 18in at 28lb to 38lb (38cm to 46cm at 13kg to 17kg), down to the present Standard's 14in to 16in (35cm to 41cm) at 28lb to 38lb. This reduction of height while retaining the weight applied also to the bitches.

In July 1952 a meeting convened in Birmingham attended by three delegates of the now seven Breed Clubs. By 12 votes to 8, an amendment to the 1948 height and weight ratio was passed. It read:

| Desired height: Dogs 16in | Desired height: Bitches 15in |
| Desired weight: Dogs 38lb. | Desired weight: Bitches 34lb. |

To us, this was a most sensible change in the Standard and one that would have taken us to a more uniform and typical breed.

After three months' delay, a report of the Meeting and majority decision was sent to The Kennel Club, who agreed to accept this amendment to the Standard. However, objections were made to The Kennel Club by the Staffordshire Bull Terrier Club and the North Western Staffordshire Bull Terrier Club. The Kennel Club reversed its decision, stating the majority vote of 12 to 8 was insufficient. When pressed, the Kennel Club would give no ruling on what would constitute a 'sufficient' majority vote.

There the matter has rested for the last thirty-four years, with the result that compressing an 18in dog of 38lb to a 16in dog at the same weight has produced a Staffordshire Bull Terrier showing far more Bull characteristics, and whatever amount of terrier influence there might have been has effectively been eliminated.

Thus we conclude that the dog created the 1935 Standard and the revised 1948 Standard created the dog; it is clear that the authors considered only the visual appearance they desired with little or no consideration for the anatomical anomalies that would result.

The pre-war bitch, Brinstock Beryl, obviously a terrier type if compared to present-day winners.

We know the origin of the Staffordshire Bull Terrier derived from a cross of Bulldog and terrier and, from recorded history, the Bulldog construction and influence was the greater. What terrier contribution there was, the 1948 Standard sufficiently diluted it to change the construction and produce the present-day specimen.

Our modern dogs have far more Bulldog in their composition than was the case years ago. Many Staffordshire Bull Terrier enthusiasts remember with great and possibly nostalgic affection the long-dead dogs of our early years in the breed and undoubtedly some deeply regret the great decrease of the influence of the terrier ancestry in this breed. However, the fact remains that our modern dog is now much more allied to the Regency-type Bulldog than to any terrier, ancient or modern.

We urge all Staffordshire Bull Terrier enthusiasts to consider carefully the arguments we put forward in favour of changing the Group classification of our breed. This we know is a very controversial suggestion but any comparison of photographs of pre-1939 winning dogs with the present successful exhibits makes it quite apparent that the terrier content of today's Staffordshire Bull Terrier has decreased enormously. We do know that the opinion of the now very few original owners and breeders we have been able to discuss this with, all consider the modern dog to be far too 'cloddy' to be considered typical of the dog with the correct blend of Bull and terrier.

As long ago as 1948, H.N. Beilby, in his highly prized book *The Staffordshire Bull Terrier*, asserted that breeders were not paying enough attention to the activity and agility of the breed. That was his opinion forty years ago and it is interesting to contemplate what his thoughts would be if he were able to spectate at a present-day show. It is certainly true that Bill Boylan, one of the most eminent of the pioneers of the breed, considered the modern dog to be immobile, phlegmatic and dull compared to his conception of the ideal Staffordshire Bull Terrier.

Should we then be judged as a Terrier in the Breed Ring and Group Ring? By virtue of the anatomic construction, the Staffordshire Bull Terrier movement cannot be likened to the movement of any other terrier, which alone will obviously preclude consideration for inclusion in the Terrier arena for this breed, without the added obvious differences in body structure.

We are and have been for too long the Cinderella breed in this Group and it is our opinion that this lack of recognition does not rest with the judges. We are expecting the Group judge to choose the best apple in the barrel and give the honour to an orange! The Terrier Breed judge and the Terrier Group judge are looking for the specimen nearest the ideal and accepted concept of a terrier. In our opinion it cannot be the Staffordshire Bull Terrier.

Our conclusion from our lengthy study of this breed is that either we battle Mother Nature for many years to conform to the accepted terrier construction or put the breed where it belongs in Non-Sporting (USA), Utility (UK) with its major ancestor the illustrious Bulldog. The name can be changed to that reported in *The Sporting Magazine* (1822): 'The Staffordshire Bulldog'. If not, we can only suggest breeders of the Staffordshire Bull Terrier love punishment in the pursuit of a seemingly impossible dream in the show ring!

2

The Breed Standard

The original Standard was written in 1935 to facilitate the entry of the breed into The Kennel Club Stud Book, and was based on two dogs regarded, at that time, to be the most typical representatives of the breed. In 1948 the Standard was revised, and was used throughout the world, with the exception of the United States where a few minor points were changed, which will be noted. We have no doubt that the 1948 revision was based on what was considered to be the desired conformation of the breed.

In 1987 the English Kennel Club issued a Breed Standard which has two additional clauses to the 1948 Standard plus some amendments, and is, we hope, a Standard that will be acceptable to all Kennel Clubs. However, it still is not anatomically easy for the breeder or the judge to comply with the directives of the Standard, as we will find there are so many anomalies in the specified structure that we have yet to attain total type. This became very apparent to the American fanciers of the late sixties and early seventies when the breed was introduced in significant numbers. They will well remember that when Staffordshire Bull Terriers were gathered together in a group, the question from onlookers was always the same: 'Are they all the same breed of dog?'. This was not the result of the breeding abilities of the American fanciers, as all those early dogs were imports from other countries, primarily the UK, and were good foundation stock.

Every member of the canine family has an identical basic anatomy, and the difference in types of breed results from the manner in which the bone structure and muscle are combined to complete those anatomical requirements that make the animal a dog. As an example, necks can be long or short, but all have the same number of vertebrae, and only the spacing, size, and proportion of bone differ.

The Standard did describe the breed as an 'all-purpose' dog, a clause which has been omitted in the 1987 revision, but in fact the

Ch. Freden Dominate. A typical example of the breed, bred by Mr Fred Holden.

Staffordshire Bull Terrier is, and must always be regarded as, an all-purpose family dog. The only reference to the purpose is 'from past history' but no additional explanation of that history exists, or why the cross of Bull and terrier was made and in what proportion. It is, at best, only conjecture. This breed competes in the Terrier Group, but is it really a terrier?

We believe that to understand what makes the Staffordshire Bull Terrier the dog we see outwardly, we must look deeper to understand the original purpose. Build and locomotion is dependent on bone structure and muscle. It is important to remember that what we do *not* see when viewing the dog is as important as what we *do* see.

In the quest to discover, through the bone structure, the original purpose and what constitutes the desired specimen for that purpose, we shall discuss individual parts of the entire body, as much as possible in the order in which they appear in the Standard. We would like the reader to bear in mind that each part of the dog is attached to the other parts and each affects both the movement and appearance of the whole. Movement, it seems, is the least understood feature of this breed and a section will be devoted to it.

For our exploration of this breed, we have used as a model a male Staffordshire Bull Terrier, examined by qualified and knowledgeable judges of this breed from Australia, USA and UK, all of whom have deemed him to be an excellent specimen with many virtues and,

Two fit and agile winners, Ch. Eastaff Noire Fill and Chewbacca the Wookie.

like all dogs, faults. He is owned by one author and bred by the other which enables us to give frank and fearless opinions, particularly as this dog will not compete in the show ring again. Extensive X-rays have been taken of the model and from these the bone structure has, as accurately as is possible, been drawn by an illustrator and reproduced in this book, together with corresponding photographs of the model. These photographs, although isolated from any unnecessary background, are otherwise scrupulously untouched (*see* page 40).

We have seriously studied the anatomy of the Staffordshire Bull Terrier but are in no way experts in that field and qualified advice has been sought when we have been unable to answer our own questions. We have related the anatomy of the Staffordshire Bull Terrier only to the extent of simple explanation of the basic structure in our effort to discover the original purpose and an explanation of the requirements of the Standard of the Breed. We leave the readers to study the anatomy more extensively as they wish.

Hindquarters, short hocks and good bend of stifle indicate long, strong musculation.

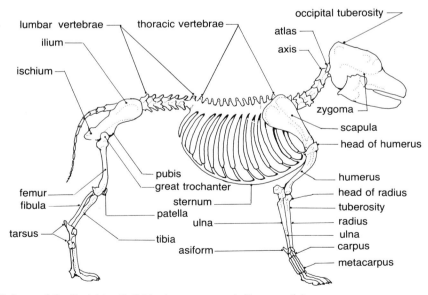

Skeleton of Staffordshire Bull Terrier, a mesocephalic type of dog. Structure drawn from X-ray photographs of our model dog (see above photograph).

The UK Breed Standard
(Reproduced by kind permission of the Kennel Club of Great Britain)

General Appearance

Well balanced, compact, exceptionally strong and muscular. Active and agile.

Characteristics

Traditionally of indomitable courage and tenacity. Highly intelligent and affectionate, especially with children.

Temperament

Bold and fearless. Totally reliable.

Head and Skull

Short, deep through with broad skull. Very pronounced cheek muscles, distinct stop, short foreface, black nose.

Eyes

Dark preferred, but may bear some relation to coat colour. Round, of medium size, and set to look straight ahead.

Ears

Rose or half-pricked, not large. Full, drop or prick, highly undesirable.

Mouth

Lips tight and clean. Jaws strong, with a perfect, regular, and complete scissor bite, i.e., upper teeth closely overlapping the lower teeth, and set square to the jaw.

41

Neck

Muscular, rather short, clean in outline, gradually widening towards the shoulders.

Forequarters

Legs straight and well boned, set rather wide apart, without looseness at the shoulders, and showing no weakness at the pasterns, from which point the feet turn out a little.

Body

Close coupled, with level topline, wide front, deep brisket, well-sprung ribs, rather light in loins.

Hindquarters

Well muscled, hocks well let down with stifles well bent. Legs parallel when viewed from behind.

Feet

Well padded, strong, and of medium size.

Tail

Medium length, low set, tapering to a point and carried rather low. Should not curl much, and may be likened to an old-fashioned pump handle.

Gait

Free, powerful and agile with economy of effort. Legs moving parallell when viewed from front or rear. Discernible drive from hind legs.

Coat

Short, smooth and close.

Colour

Red, fawn, white, black or blue, or any of these colours with white. Any shade of brindle, or any shade of brindle with white. Black and tan or liver colour not to be encouraged.

Height & Weight

Weight: Dogs 28lb to 38lb; bitches 24lb to 34lb. Height (at shoulder): 14 to 16 inches, these heights being related to the weights.

Faults

Any departure from the foregoing points should be considered a fault, and the seriousness with which the fault should be regarded should be in exact proportion to its degree.

Notes

Male animals should have two apparently normal testicles fully descended into the scrotum.

The USA Breed Standard

(Reproduced by kind permission of the
American Kennel Club)

Characteristics

From the past history of the Staffordshire Bull Terrier, the modern dog draws its character of indomitable courage, high intelligence, and tenacity. This, coupled with its affection for its friends, and children in particular, its off-duty quietness and trustworthy stability, makes it a foremost all-purpose dog.

General Appearance

The Staffordshire Bull Terrier is a smooth-coated dog. It should be of great strength for its size and, although muscular, should be active and agile.

Head and Skull

Short, deep through with broad skull, very pronounced cheek muscles, distinct stop, short foreface, black nose. Pink (Dudley) nose to be considered a serious fault.

Eyes

Dark preferable, but may bear some relation to coat color. Round, of medium size, and set to look straight ahead. Light eyes or pink eye rims to be considered a fault, except that where the coat surrounding the eye is white the eye rim may be pink.

Ears

Rose or half-pricked, not large. Full drop or full prick to be considered a serious fault.

Mouth

A bite in which the outer side of the lower incisors touches the inner side of the upper incisors. The lips should be tight and clean. The badly undershot or overshot bite is a serious fault.

Neck

Muscular, rather short, clean in outline and gradually widening towards the shoulders.

Forequarters

Legs straight and well boned, set rather far apart, without looseness at the shoulders and showing no weakness at the pasterns, from which point the feet turn out a little.

Body

The body is close coupled, with a level topline, wide front, deep brisket and well-sprung ribs being rather light in the loins.

Hindquarters

The hindquarters should be well muscled, hocks let down with stifles well bent. Legs should be parallel when viewed from behind.

Feet

The feet should be well padded, strong and of medium size. Dewclaws, if any, on the hind legs are generally removed. Dewclaws on the forelegs may be removed.

Tail

The tail is undocked, of medium length, low set, tapering to a point and carried rather low. It should not curl much and may be likened to an old-fashioned pump handle. A tail that is too long or badly curled is a fault.

Coat

Smooth, short and close to the skin, not to be trimmed or dewhiskered.

Colour

Red, fawn, white, black or blue, or any of these colors with white. Any shade of brindle or any shade of brindle with white. Black-and-tan or liver color to be disqualified.

Size

Weight: Dogs, 28 to 38 pounds; bitches, 24 to 34 pounds. Height at shoulder: 14 to 16 inches, these heights being related to weights. Non-conformity with these limits is a fault.

Disqualifications

Black-and-tan or liver color.

This dog exemplifies the correct present-day breed type.

Discussion of the UK and USA Breed Standards

General Appearance

Active and agile   This is very important since it is the only part of the Standard which can possibly be construed as including reference to the locomotion of the breed. The judge, under the Standard, has absolutely no obligation to take notice of movement as long as in his opinion the dog is 'active and agile'.

In the absence of information on movement in the Standard and since the breed is classified as a terrier, it will be judged on terrier movement and here we meet our first problem. Is the breed a true terrier and can it, with its present conformation, move as a true terrier? We cannot answer that until we have thoroughly examined the dog in its entirety.

Head

UK: Short deep through, broad skull, very pronounced cheek muscles, distinct stop, short foreface, black nose.
USA: Short deep through, broad skull, very pronounced cheek muscles, distinct stop, short foreface, black nose. Pink (Dudley) Nose to be considered a serious fault.

The late H.N. Beilby, one of the founding fathers of this breed, wrote that, in his opinion, 'skull and ears are that of the bulldog, while the muzzle is strengthened and jaw levelled by the introduction of the terriers'.

Old prints tend to show that the extremely short muzzle of the present-day Bulldog is a show feature which has been bred into it over a period of years. Indeed, the head of the present-day Staffordshire Bull Terrier more closely resembles drawings of the old-type Bulldog than it does any terrier breed. The width and depth of skull, coupled with the rose ears, is very definitely a Bulldog feature, and the distinct stop with required round eyes are features by which a Bulldog was recognized in early days.

These features show a marked leaning toward 'Bull' rather than 'terrier' ancestry of the Staffordshire Bull Terrier. This can be seen from the drawing illustrating the old Bulldog which came from an

This dog has that alert and interested expression typical of a good Staffordshire Bull Terrier.

interesting book by William Youatt entitled *The Dog* (1851), printed 'Under the Superintendence of the Society for the Diffusion of Useful Knowledge'.

Dogs were grouped in Divisions and, under the Third Division of the Varieties of Dog, the author writes:

> . . . the muzzle more or less shortened, the front sinus enlarged and the cranium elevated and diminished in capacity. At the head of this inferior and brutal Division of Dogs stands the Bulldog. The round thick head, turned-up nose and thick and pendulous lips of this dog are familiar to all, while his ferocity makes him in the highest degree dangerous.

Following the head of this Division is the 'Bull and Terrier' which, of course, is the earliest emergence of the Staffordshire Bull Terrier. Here the author writes:

> This cross is between the bulldog and terrier and is generally

superior, both in appearance and value, to either of its progenitors. A second cross considerably lessens the underhanging of the lower jaw, and a third entirely removes it, retaining the spirit and determination of the animals.

To us, the interesting part is the 'muzzle more or less shortened' description of the bulldog. From the many old drawings and pictures we have seen in our research for this book, the bulldog undoubtedly was 'short in the foreface' and the present-day Bulldog has a far greater protuberance of the lower jaw rostal to the upper jaw, seeming to confirm that the foreface of the present-day Bulldog has greatly decreased in length. The length and description, coupled with the drawing, appears much more in likeness to the present-day Staffordshire Bull Terrier, keeping in mind that the Bulldog always, it seems, featured the undershot condition.

Usually, by continuous selective breeding, the union of a very short-faced brachycephalic breed, such as the Bulldog, with a long-faced dolichocephalic breed, produces the mid-length foreface of the mesocephalic. From early drawings, the Bulldog then appeared more mesocephalic and is now brachycephalic, and to us it appears that the Staffordshire Bull Terrier has also, over the past fifty years, become a little shorter in foreface than the average mesocephalic head, doubtless through fashion breeding.

When considering the length of foreface and length of skull, research into head proportion of the most typical Staffordshire Bull Terriers shows the desired length of skull to foreface to be two to one. That is, if the length of head from the occiput to the stop is divided by the distance from the stop of the nostrils, the ideal ratio is that the skull is twice as long as the foreface. This has been accepted over the years by judges and breeders alike as a yardstick of ratio even though it is not so stated in the Standard. We feel it would be well for breeders to keep to this ratio since any further shortening of the foreface, coupled with the deep stop, will lead us eventually from mesocephalic to brachycephalic with all the disease problems of the soft and hard palates and breathing difficulties resulting from misshapen nasal bones. The ratio of two to one that we now have enables the dog to hold a bite without inhibiting breathing ability.

The skull, which includes the cranium, is very complex and, for the purpose of understanding the prime feature we desire in the head, we concentrate on a very limited explanation. The head of the

Truestaff Orchid Challenger (right) and Barkers Bullseye Abominog (below). They have different heads but both are correct and of good type. It is a matter of individual choice which you prefer.

Eastaff Lil' Stotter. Note the short foreface and the strength of the underjaw.

Staffordshire Bull Terrier must be positive, but should never be considered as a separate entity, and should always balance with the structure of the dog. The old saying, 'there is more behind the collar than there is in front' is, indeed, still well worth keeping uppermost in mind when viewing the dog.

The head is deep and wide with a clearly defined sagittal crest, the ridge down the centre of the skull from occiput to the stop, formed by the fusion of the parietal bones. The crest provides protection for the cranium and a surface for the attachment of one of the largest and strongest head muscles, the temporal muscle. The temporal arises from the overlying recess of the parietal bone and to a lesser extent the temporal, frontal and occipital bones and extends to the coronoid process of the mandible (lower jaw). The function of the temporal muscle is to raise and retract the lower jaw and to hold the mouth closed. The mandible is almost straight from its erect posterior angle forward to the incisors. The two halves of the lower jaw (rami) join in the middle incisors, being almost completely together by the time the dog is mature.

Another important muscle is the masseter, which arises from the medial surface of the zygomatic arch and attaches to the entire vertical portion of the mandible. It is responsible for retracting the lower jaw and also for lateral movement. The strong development of this muscle gives the much desired feature of well-pronounced cheek muscles. The strength of bite and ability to lock is provided by the temporal and masseter muscles but the bite strength is also dependent upon the cutting molars being well set in their foundations in each jaw. A most important feature when viewing the head is the fill-in in front of the eyes, indicating proper anchorage for the molars. It seems seldom that this is noticed or regarded with much interest. The temporal muscle lies below the skin of the forehead on each side of the crest and helps to shape the head.

The breadth of head depends upon the development, width and curvature of the zygomatic arch which is a lateral bridge of bone linking the neural and facial areas of the skull. Three separate bones, the malar, frontal and lachrymal bones, make up the zygoma. The arch of the zygoma is attached to the temporal bone towards the back of the skull and in front to the maxilla, and it delineates the open space of the orbit.

The orbital cavity is divided into two parts: a larger posterior section and a lesser frontal portion which is formed by the inner edges of the frontal bone, partly encasing the eye. However, the eyeball is not completely enclosed as it would be by a socket. Although the orbit is open at approximately mid-way, there is a tubercle (small protuberance) on the inner edge of the frontal bone opposite a similar tubercle on the inner edge of the zygoma. A fibrous ligament joins these tubercles and effectively divides the orbit into the front ocular portion and a posterior temporal portion. The coronoid process of the mandible moves freely in the orbit through the temporal portion when the mouth is opened and closed.

The pronounced stop, of considerable influence in the desired shape of the head and its prominence, is shaped by frontal sinuses. These are two air chambers lying one on each side of the head above the eye within the frontal bones. The stop separates the forehead from the nasal passages. The angle between the cranium

Ch. Cradbury Flash Danny Boy. Note the developed cheek muscles and the strength of the jaw.

Rigel Dominator. Note the angle of the foreface to the skull.

and foreface is referred to as the cranio-facial angle. The overdeveloped stop, which we are apt to admire in our breed, may increase the chance of breeding deformities of the palate and other respiratory disorders.

The nostrils are seldom viewed with much interest other than the Standard's directive that they should be black. The Standard gives no guidance on width or size and we consider that this breed, because of the short foreface and attendant reduction in length of nasal bones, should have large wide nostrils to ensure good breathing capacity.

For the good head we desire, foreface and skull must be parallel with each other and never be downfaced. There can be no compromise on this point.

Comparing the head of the Staffordshire Bull Terrier with that of the American Pitbull Terrier, there is little likeness in structure or appearance. The AMPT Standard calls for the forehead to be brick-shaped, which means longer in length and with more squareness of the skull. Pronounced cheeks, free from wrinkles, are required and the muzzle should be square, wide and deep with well-pronounced jaws, displaying strength. The skull is not as broad as that of the Staffordshire Bull Terrier. No indication is given of a ratio between skull and foreface but from observation the foreface is longer than that of the Staffordshire Bull Terrier and is brick-shaped, as is the skull. Ears are cropped closely to the skull, as would be expected for a fighting dog, since overly large and drooping ears would probably be the first to be injured.

We believe the foreface of the Staffordshire Bull Terrier is far too short for the purpose of dog-fighting and would have been better suited to bull-baiting. The tremendous biting power is ideal for locking onto a bull's nose, rather than a required fast change of bite for a more advantageous hold which would be required in dog-fighting. Both these breeds have the great ability to lock onto a bite but the ability to change bite quickly would be of little use to a dog being tossed around in mid-air while the inability to change bite quickly for a better hold would spell disaster for the dog in the pit.

Eyes

UK: Dark preferably but may bear some relation to coat colour. Round of medium size and set to look straight ahead. To be penalized – light eyes or pink eye rims.
USA: Dark preferably but may bear some relation to coat colour. Round of medium size and set to look straight ahead. Light eyes or pink eye rims to be considered a fault, except that where the coat surrounding the eye is white, the eye rim may be pink.

As the width of the skull greatly depends upon the curvature of the zygomatic arch, so does the size and capacity of the open orbit housing the eyes. The straighter the arch, the more oblique are the eyes in relation to the skull centre.

A pad of fat keeps the eye in position and acts as a buffer against eye injury. The support of this pad retains the eyeball accurately in position in relation to the space between the eyelids. This is one very obvious area where the health of the dog is instantly apparent since an undernourished animal will lose fat from the fat pad which, in turn, is then unable to support the eye correctly, and the eyes appear to sink into the head.

Ch. Redstaff King, showing good eye placement.

The eyeball is not a perfect sphere and measures slightly more from front to back than vertically. The cornea, in the centre, is the transparent part of the eyeball which allows light to penetrate into the interior of the eye. The globe of the eyeball behind the cornea is comprised of three layers: the sclera lies outside the choroid which is lined by the sensitive retina. The optic nerve penetrates the sclera and spreads out in branches inside the eye over the retina. Within the retina are layers of glistening cells which cause the eyes to shine when they are caught in a bright light.

There are two eyelids, the upper and the lower, together with a third eyelid called the membrana nictitans which is located in the inner (medial) corner of the eye. This third lid moves very quickly across the eye to protect the cornea and helps distribute tears over the cornea surface to keep it moist and remove foreign material from the eye. The eyelids are lined by a moist membrane, the conjuctiva, which is continuous with the sclera.

The Standard calls for the eyes to be 'round and of medium size'.

Since the eyeball itself is not totally round, this is obtained by the spacing of the eyelids. The eyes are 'set to look straight ahead', giving almost forward vision; this is provided by the zygomatic arch curvature and a peri-orbital cushion of fatty tissue. Separate sets of muscle control movement of the eyes within the orbital cavity.

Under the Standard, eyes are required to be preferably dark but may bear some relation to the coat colour. The dark eye is more attractive and to a degree is a cosmetic feature, although it does give guidance to retention or loss of pigmentation.

Presumably, the directive that colour may bear some relation to the coat colour is for fawn-coated dogs. Relative colour for the white Staffordshire Bull Terrier must be a matter of conjecture and personal judgement. It is generally accepted that the eyes should be dark.

The UK Standard calls for a fault on pink eye rims. The USA Standard adds, 'except that where the coat surrounding the eye is white, the eye rim may be pink'. The present-day fanciers in the USA who have successfully bred and shown white-headed dogs must be grateful for that change in the Standard, and acknowledgement for it is entirely due to Mr Steve Stone who had the foresight to suggest this inclusion.

No matter what colour the eye, it has no bearing on the quality of the dog's sight. The colour of the 'eye' in fact results from the pigment cells in the iris – a diaphragm which opens and closes to control the amount of light passing through the eye to reach the retina. An absence of pigment results in a pale iris or 'wall eye' and this may interfere with the ability to control light and, therefore, influence sight.

The light entering the eye is focused by the lens which lies behind the iris. This lens can become dislocated and lose its clarity in cataract. Both conditions may result in blindness.

Ears

UK: Rose or half-pricked and not large. Full drop or full prick to be penalized.
USA: Rose or half-pricked and not large. Full drop or full prick to be considered a serious fault.

We do not find it necessary to analyze the function and construction of the ear as a hearing organ. Suffice to say it is an extremely complex organ, consisting of three parts – external, middle and inner – and ear problems should be left strictly in the care of a veterinary surgeon.

However, the physical appearance of the ears is extremely important and contributes greatly to the overall appearance of the head. Poor ears can almost ruin the appearance of what may be quite a reasonable head. A judge will often forgive a fault in body, even construction, but rarely will a specimen with poor ears be considered. There is no disqualification for incorrect ear shape, and therefore a dog with poor ear shape and carriage is not precluded from entry into the ring. However, the Standard gives no indication of carriage and placement. The best example we have found is shown in the photograph below, where the ears are correctly rosed and set well apart almost on the side of the head.

It appears to us that the half-prick ear is caused by the fact that the ear is too short in length for the base-width and, although this type of ear gives whelps a good-looking head, with growth and development of muscle the ear will very likely be full-prick in the

Curfew's Badger Bill. Note the neat ears correctly carried.

adult specimen. The half-prick ear usually is too high in carriage to be accepted.

The heredity factors for heavy and drop ears seem to remain from generation to generation and however much concentration one gives to this factor when breeding, it will recur from time to time. Sensible breeders should make sure that the stud of their choice, or bitch for the stud, has good ears and, moreover, that the required ear was a feature of the forebears.

The heavy and full drop ear is a much greater problem and from experience is much more difficult to breed out.

Although the Breed Standard does not specify thickness of ears, it is desired that they should be thin.

Dentition (Mouth)

UK: The mouth should be level, i.e. the incisors of the bottom jaw should fit closely inside the incisors of the top jaw, and the lips should be tight and clean. The badly undershot or overshot mouth to be heavily penalized.

USA: A bite in which the outer side of the lower incisors touches the inner side of the upper incisors. The lips should be tight and clean. The badly undershot or overshot bite is a serious fault.

Colour of eyes is often regarded as a cosmetic feature. Dentition is not a cosmetic feature and is totally related to soundness. The prehensile organ of the family Candiae is the mouth and the only way it can survive is if it is used to catch, kill and consume.

The number of teeth, their shape and size, coupled with the head muscles governing the strength of bite that we have already discussed, are Nature's creation to enable the dog to survive; they serve as defensive weapons and are not intended for winning a beauty contest. The obvious fact that the domestic dog is no longer responsible for his own welfare does not mean that the gums and teeth should not be healthy and sound from puppyhood through to old age.

Invariably, the inspection of the dentition by judges involves parting the lips and examining the incisors to ensure the bite is correct as required by the Standard. Neither the Standard nor the limited time allotted provides any obligation to examine further. It seems that breeders examining a prospective stud, or stud owners a bitch, seldom give more than cursory inspection to the dentition.

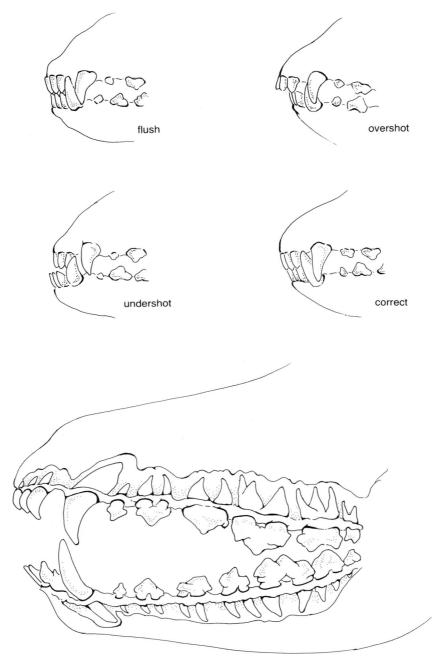

flush

overshot

undershot

correct

Dentition of the Staffordshire Bull Terrier.

The interest is focused on the requirement of the show ring to ensure a correct scissor bite. It is doubtful whether pet owners examine for this at all.

The natural bite of the dog is the scissor bite of the incisors behind which the remaining teeth of the upper and lower jaws also have to work in harmony. With the obvious emphasis focused almost exclusively upon the incisor bite, the total bite is invariably ignored yet is of greater importance to the health and welfare of the dog and the breed. There are some fanciers and breeders and, we might add, judges, who are not particularly concerned by the undershot condition and they must realize that internal soundness should never take second place to the outward appearance.

When the length of the foreface is shortened in the dog such as in our breed, the reduction is obtained in the jaws, particularly the upper jaw, and this will inevitably cause a distortion or deviation of tooth placement in both upper and lower jaws. When we eat, our digestive system obliges us to masticate food into a pulp before it is swallowed, and our teeth are designed to aid in this process. The

Ch. Teutonic Warrior. Note the good strong dentition and underjaw.

dog's digestive system enables it to bolt its food in larger pieces so that the teeth are not required to break food down to the same degree. Before domestication of the dog, to protect its kill, eating quickly by bolting down large pieces was the rule, and guarding food by growling off another dog is often still exhibited between pet dogs in the home. However, the dentition cannot function as intended if tooth relationships are disturbed, as in the over or undershot jaws, and incorrect tooth alignment leads to difficulties in mastication and ultimately loss of teeth.

There are four types of teeth, each having a separate function. Incisors are for tearing skin and meat off the bone, canines aid in catching, holding and killing the prey, premolars shear off and chew muscle meat and molars cut meat and splinter bone. Molars and premolars are frequently referred to as shearing or cheek teeth.

Puppies have 28 teeth, called deciduous or baby teeth, the formula for which is: I – 3/3; C – 1/1; PM – 3/3, upper and lower, each side of the mouth. From this you will observe that there are no molars. The deciduous teeth are replaced by the permanent teeth so that the adult dog possesses 42 permanent teeth: I – 3/3; C – 1/1; PM – 4/4; M – 2/3, upper and lower, each side of the mouth.

The teeth are arranged in upper and lower dental arcades, the lower being narrower and shorter. Each tooth is divided into three parts: the crown which is covered by white enamel and exposed above the gumline, the neck located at the gumline, and the root, below the gumline, anchored in sockets in the jaws (alveoli).

Incisors The upper incisor roots are anchored in the incisive and maxillary bones and, for a correct scissor bite, are slightly forward of the lower incisors. If the upper incisors close behind the lower this is known as prognathism of the mandible, i.e. the undershot condition. This condition can also occur not only as a result of increase in length of the mandible but also by reduction in its width, so that the lower incisor roots become too crowded and the crowns are forced to 'flare out' as they grow and so come to lie in the front of the upper incisors.

Canines These are the longest teeth and are separated by a space from the corner incisors so that when the mouth is closed, the lower canine can lie forward of the upper. The canines of the upper jaw are usually slightly larger than the lower but both have long roots which are almost twice the length of the exposed tooth.

Premolars These are often referred to as cheek teeth and lie immediately behind the canines. The first is small with a peg-like root. The second and third in both jaws are identical and have two roots each. The fourth premolars of the upper jaw are the largest cutting teeth and are the carnassial teeth, often referred to as shearing teeth. They have three conical roots. The fourth premolars of the lower jaw are much smaller, each with two roots.

Molars These are also known as cheek teeth and lie behind the premolars. There are two molars each side of the upper jaw and three each side of the lower jaw. The molars of the upper jaw and the second and third molars of the lower jaw are quite small. The first molar of the lower jaw is large and referred to as the carnassial tooth of the lower jaw and matches the carnassial tooth (fourth premolar) of the upper jaw.

Teeth must be strong and of good size in this breed, but it appears to us that they are becoming both smaller and weaker, thus losing any advantage gained by breeding strong head muscles to give a good bite. This would be a great disadvantage in a breed required to perform either in the pit or bull-baiting. However, the Standard gives no reference to the size of the teeth.

The UK Standard calls for a scissor bite – or does it? It is clearly defined in the USA Standard but there is somewhat ambiguous wording in the UK Standard which states, 'the mouth should be level i.e. incisors of the lower jaw should fit closely inside the incisors of the top jaw'. It is poor wording to say 'the mouth should be level' and then add 'i.e.' and then proceed with a clear description of a scissor bite.

The *level* or *flush* mouth is when the cutting edges of the incisors meet edge to edge. The 1987 KC amendment has clarified this, and is now a clear and understandable directive. *Wry* means the incisors on one side of the mouth are undershot and the opposite side scissor bite. *Undershot* is when the lower incisors protrude outside the upper incisors. *Overshot* is the opposite of undershot where the upper incisors are so well forward of the lower incisors they do not fit closely and a gap is created.

Regrettably, our main problem has always appeared to be the undershot mouth. We agree that it be counted as a single fault when judging an otherwise excellent specimen, but we must take into account that the mouth is not a cosmetic feature, and breed history clearly shows that the undershot condition is the easiest to produce and takes no effort to maintain in this breed. The correct bite, i.e. scissor, is of paramount importance in permanent dentition. Overshot, undershot, flush and wry are invariably associated with mismatched length of jaws leading to misplacement of canines, premolars and molars. We believe that anything other than a scissor bite should be severely penalized by judges and given far more attention in breeding programmes. Strength of jaws, so admired and desired in this breed, becomes but a cosmetic feature if the dentition is weak, misplaced and, therefore, unsound.

Unfortunately, as many long-time fanciers have learned, a perfect scissor bite in this breed cannot be guaranteed, particularly in puppies at the time of placing in homes. In fact, it can and usually does take up to ten months before one is sure the dentition is correct, and even then it seldom lasts through to advanced years in the Staffordshire Bull Terrier.

It is one of the anomalies of this breed that the Standard requires the dog to have a short foreface, very strong jaws and scissor bite, three factors which, to a large extent, are opposed to each other. However, all three features must be sought after since a large, well-shaped and proportioned head must be correct in all its aspects. It then behoves us diligently to tackle the problem of ridding the breed of its propensity toward poor dentition by the undershot condition and to strive for the correct scissor bite. It is in the hands of the breeder since it starts with the mating.

Neck

UK and USA: Muscular, rather short, clean in outline and gradually widening towards the shoulders.

The Standard gives a very clear and concise picture of the correct neck structure of the Staffordshire Bull Terrier and it seems a feature well retained. The neck is a very important part of construction as it has a vital bearing on the carriage and movement of the animal. Invariably, the head and neck are related to one another in length, i.e. short-headed breeds will have short necks, and this is certainly true of this breed. Carriage of the head affects balance and movement. With the head lowered the scapulae become more upright and the front leg movement automatically becomes very short and generally shows less purpose.

Ch. Tridwr Dicey Riley. Note the strong neck leading to a good shoulder structure.

A dog requires a length of head and neck which allows the animal's nose and mouth to reach the ground without being forced to assume a 'stooped' position. Should the short neck be coupled with shoulder blades of 45 degrees the dog would not be able to get his head down to the floor and would tip forward. This is not conjecture but fact, deduced from X-rays of our model and our extensive examination of a great many Staffordshire Bull Terriers.

The neck has seven vertebrae. The first two (atlas and axis) allow free head movement and differ considerably in shape and size from the remaining five. The point where the atlas and axis join the remaining five divides the neck into two parts with separate sets of muscles. The point of union is shown by a pronounced curve of the arch of the neckline and is the crest or poll of the neck. From the crest or poll of the neck forward, the two vertebrae (atlas and axis) have muscles attached each side which connect with the upper arm and draw it forward.

65

The higher the head is carried the more these muscles tend to lift the front action. As the dog goes forward the head is lowered slightly so that the pull of the muscles is more specially in the line of travel. These are also the muscles the dog uses to shake his prey. Obviously, if the dog has good muscular neck development with a well-defined crest, better control of front movement is obtained.

The cervical ligament (*ligamentum nuchae*) is of paramount importance to the efficient working of the neck. It extends from the axis to the dorsal (thoracic) vertebrae and, unlike other ligaments, it has an elasticated contractile ability. To a very large extent, it supports the neck and so controls the head carriage. It also provides a stable base for the attachment of the muscles that move the leg forward. Weakness in the neck ligament will result in little support for the muscles moving the front leg forward. The short neck of the Staffordshire Bull Terrier does reduce the length and efficient working of muscles controlling the shoulder blade, with consequent reduction in the possible forward movement of the front leg.

A short neck, properly muscled, is a strong neck which would be totally necessary to withstand the shock of severe tossing for a dog who has the bull by the nose and where little forward movement would be required.

The American Pitbull Terrier neck is long and entirely necessary for the pursuit of dog fighting in that the dog must have length of neck to move the head around to defend himself in the rear without undue turning of the body. The bull-baiting dog, once he had a hold, would have to hang on regardless of being strongly tossed about, and a long neck would more easily be injured. It is, therefore, apparent that this part of the Breed Standard could not have been conceived if the dog was considered a good prospect for the pit as its original purpose.

Forequarters

UK and USA: Legs straight and well boned, set rather far apart, without looseness at the shoulders and showing no weakness at the pasterns, from which point the feet turn out a little.

The very sparse paragraph in the Standard must be taken to describe the whole of the forequarters of the Staffordshire Bull Terrier. It is meant to, and possibly does, give a word picture of the physical appearance required. However, in no way does it explain the construction problems posed by the wording. In our breed, it is very difficult to produce physically sound animals and at the same time remain true to the anatomical structure we have to maintain. Breeders have to fight a battle with nature to produce an animal that is consistent with the Standard.

The required physical characteristics, 'legs straight and well boned', are very simple and straightforward, but this clause must be considered and coupled together with 'set rather far apart' and 'without looseness at the shoulders'. A wide front (chest cavity) requires considerable lateral angulation of the shoulder blades, and

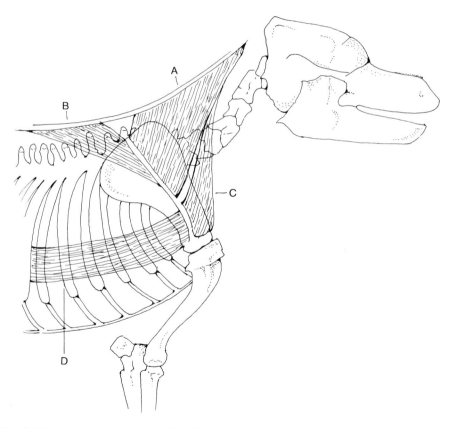

It will help to understand the shoulder blade muscles by studying the trapezius (A and B), the omotransversarius (C) and the deep pectoral (D), which work in harmonious opposition: A and D, B and C.

Placement of biceps (A) and triceps (B) which operate the elbow joint.

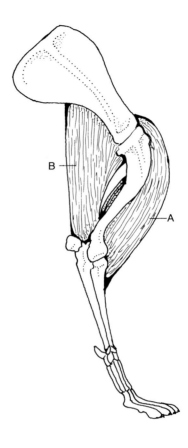

the natural stance of the dog would normally bring the pads (feet) well inward from the shoulder point in order to maintain balance. Only by accepting a more vertical shoulder blade is it possible to bring the pads under the dog and maintain the required 'legs straight' and 'set rather far apart', otherwise the breeder must be resigned to producing 'Chippendale fronts'. Additionally, the musculature of the dog has to be sufficiently strong, particularly the triceps, to hold the shoulder in with the dog balanced. Fortunately, the Standard requires the feet to turn out a little which does help to obtain balance more easily than if they were required to be front forward and in line.

Now consider 'without looseness at the shoulders'. From our own observations and from authoritative material you may read, it must

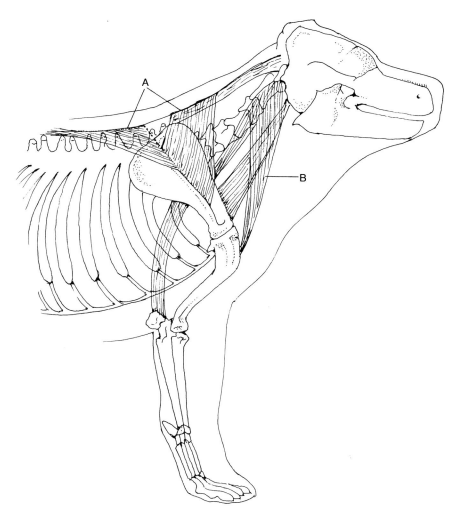

Some of the external muscles used in the forward movement of the forelegs – the trapezius (A) and the brachialis (B).

be realized that it is very difficult to have a short neck, as described in the previous section, and a shoulder blade angulation of 45 degrees (well-laid back) which, although not mentioned in the Standard, is considered by canine anatomists to be ideal, regardless of breed. If the shoulder is too upright to allow the animal to move without undue effort, the weight of the foreparts bear heavily upon

69

the humerus, which tends to swivel inwards and, in effect, turns the shoulder out.

So, in summary, we have another anomaly in the requirement of the wide front and straight legs from which it is so very easy to produce looseness and overloading of the shoulders, faults which must be severely penalized under the Standard.

The neck is an integral part of the front and all the muscles that draw the leg forward depend either directly or indirectly on the neck to provide a base for support. The weak neck indicates the inability of the neck ligament to control the break of the poll and, therefore, does not give good support to those muscles which move the front legs forward. The length of the forward stride of the forelegs, to a great extent, governs the drive that the hind legs are able to contribute to the movement of the dog, and, to maintain balance and smooth co-ordination, the forelimb motion will dictate the pattern of the movement that the hind legs have to adopt. Understandably, then, a short neck does give problems in movement.

The forelimb is pulled forward by the *levator humeri*, a long thin muscle extending from forward of the poll of the neck to the shoulder blade, biceps and the all-important brachiocephalic muscle which is fixed in front of the occipital bone at one end and at the other just below the shoulder joint of the upper arm, dictating the forelimb movement subject to the height the head is carried.

The scapula is a triangular bone whose shape enables it to cover a wide surface and provide anchorage for the muscles that operate the limbs and influence neck movement. These muscles have a vital effect on movement by their length and strength.

As well as the length of neck, the Standard also requires well-sprung ribs, and again this presents another anomaly. The angle of inclination of the scapulae is also influenced by the degree of the curvature of the first four ribs. In foreleg movement, the scapula must slide over the first four ribs. With ribs 'well sprung' or 'curved', the upper ends of the scapulae are forced further apart into a more upright position during backward motion. This is a contributing factor to the shortening of the forward reach. Additionally, the pulling outward of the upper ends of the scapulae causes the elbows to follow, so that to maintain balance the toes turn inwards, i.e. pin-toeing.

The biceps muscles which extend down the front part of the humerus from the scapula, are in some degree an extension of the

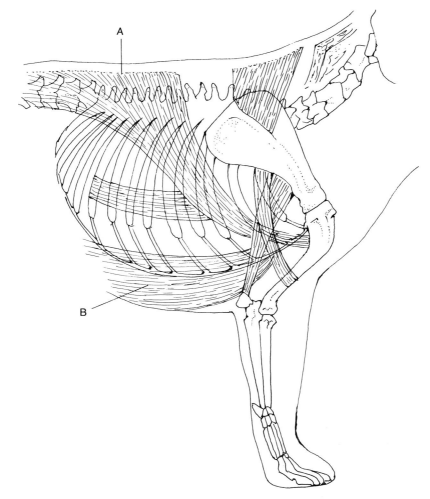

Muscles used in the backward movement of the foreleg, mainly the dorsal (A) and the pectoral (B).

brachiocephalic muscles and are used in the forward movement of the animal. They function in opposition to the complicated set of triceps muscles which lie behind the shoulder and run from the back end of the scapula to the elbow.

When watching the front movement, the leg appears to move backwards in relation to the body. However, unless the dog is

71

Ch. Silverlake Fagin, showing a good, well-developed front with correct musculation.

digging, the body in fact moves forward over the leg which is held in a static position. When the leg first contacts the ground it is braced and straight, and the first action appears almost to be of folding up or bending for an instant beneath the body, immediately followed by a retracting action. To obtain front movement, shoulder blade rotation is achieved by the front half of the trapezius muscle pulling the top of the scapula forward and the serratus muscle pulling the lower half of the blade backward.

All animals are constructed so as to display what is known in the car industry as 'independent suspension', i.e. all four 'corners' work independently but, nevertheless, in conjunction with one another to provide a smooth and effortless forward motion. We use this comparison to explain why good shoulder placement is so desirable.

When the foreleg locks at the full extent of the forward movement, the scapula and joints act in the same manner as the car's shock absorber when the front of the car goes over an obstacle in the road. This anatomical form allows the animal to continue to move forward with the least possible interference to the smoothness of its progression.

We strongly believe that strength and correct development of the forelimb and neck muscles are of tremendous importance to our breed and lack of correct musculature will result in an even shorter forward movement with the distinct possibility that the elbows would be inclined to move outward. When the scapula is too upright and the musculature is short, too much weight is carried by the elbows as the shoulders cannot provide the necessary spring to counteract the transition of weight over the forelimb. Such a conformation is extremely unsound and may result from our attempts to obtain a sympathetic balance between the anatomical peculiarities inherent in our breed. Thus, any deviation from soundness in the Staffordshire Bull Terrier must be abhorred.

It is apparent to us that if we require front movement in our breed to be comparable with terrier breeds, we must be prepared to sacrifice some of the physical properties that we have explained and which most fanciers consider desirable, or resign ourselves to the fact that this breed moves differently from that of the terrier and, from that viewpoint, differently to what is anatomically desirable.

This also applies to that part of the Standard which states that the forelimbs will show 'no weakness at the pasterns, from which point the feet turn out a little'. This is a very typical characteristic of the breed and, in our opinion, we should not try to eliminate it.

It is obvious to us, in our quest to find the breed's original purpose, that with the short neck, wide front, upright scapula and feet that turn slightly out, this breed is no dog-fighting animal. Such an animal would require a longer neck to turn around more easily on the adversary to protect its rear; need feet straight forward as it would be required to hold ground, to move forward and around and not upward; and need longer forearm construction and a greater inclination of the scapulae to allow freedom of action in the front to 'wrestle'.

The bull-baiting combatant would have the advantage of using the slightly out-turned push-off foot as leverage to purchase more ground and power for the lift-off. The dog would need to be able

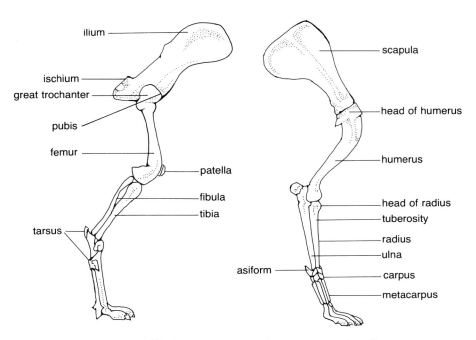

Bone structure of hind limb.   *Bone structure of forelimb.*

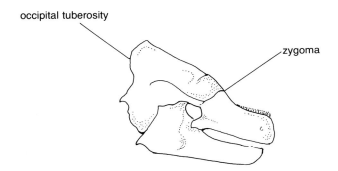

Typical mesocephalic head. (Medium length foreface).

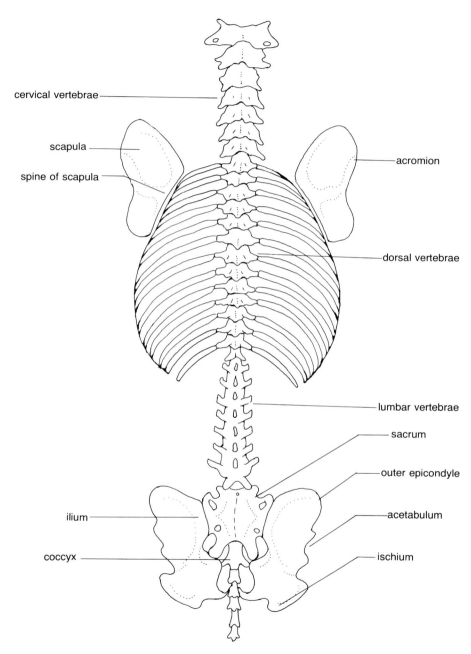

cervical vertebrae

scapula

spine of scapula

acromion

dorsal vertebrae

lumbar vertebrae

sacrum

outer epicondyle

acetabulum

ilium

coccyx

ischium

Looking down on the skeleton, this diagram illustrates the vertebrae and the relative placement of shoulders, ribs and pelvis.

75

Both these exhibits show the slight 'out turn' of the feet, which is correct in this breed.

to go upwards at any angle with great speed and accuracy in a very confined area, yet still be able to keep his body facing the bull. The bull would not have been a passive creature but would have tossed its head with great force to avoid the adversary or shake it loose. The dog would need enormous agility with a short neck of great strength that was less easy to break, as well as a wide front and a solid body to act as a pendulum.

Furthermore, with the forequarter construction as it is – large head, short neck, upright shoulders, short forward reach, out-turned feet – the Staffordshire Bull Terrier is, so far, showing us little influence from a terrier ancestor.

Body

UK and USA: The body is close coupled, with a level topline, wide front, deep brisket and well sprung ribs, being rather light in the loin.

This part of the Standard describes the physical characteristics of the whole body and provides the shape and substance of the Staffordshire Bull Terrier. We think it will make the description easier if we first point out that the body is in two parts, the thorax and the abdomen, which are separated from one another by an internal muscular partition called the diaphragm.

Strength and health depend solely upon the amount of energy supplied to all the working parts of the dog which is generated internally by various organs. It must, therefore, be quite obvious that the construction of the housing of these organs and its capacity are of vital importance. Basically, the internal organs perform the same functions for every breed. However, the structural variations of one breed may well be determined by the accent on speed and in another by endurance, but obviously a balance must be maintained since to breed for speed without endurance would have little advantage.

Construction of the body must be designed to give maximum efficiency to a dog to enable him to perform the function for which

Cottfall Princess of Tridwr. She shows good 'cut up' and length of rib cage.

77

he was bred. Without doubt, the Staffordshire Bull Terrier is bred for endurance and for the original purpose (albeit pit-fighting or bull-baiting), speed would be required, but only within a confined area from side to side, backward, forward and upward. It is said of this breed that 'it can turn on a dime'. A well-remembered performance of this ability was shown the first time we had a Best of Breed in the Terrier Group in the USA. The dog, not being able to gait further in the ring, turned with such speed that several onlookers expressed amazement that they had not actually seen him turn. This is a characteristic of the breed, and judges should, in fact, look for this agility in the show ring. The slightly turned-out feet, coupled with excellent muscular development, have a great deal to do with this ability.

The Standard gives us every opportunity for a 'workshop' that provides the space needed for the organs to give the tremendous vitality and agility we regard as typical of this breed.

Close coupled   This refers to the link between the front and back assemblies which, anatomically, is the loin, but is referred to as the coupling when assessing the length of the dog.

The length of body should be taken from the tip of the sternum to the tip of the buttock. To measure this accurately would require a measuring stick with a fixed right-angle arm at one end and a sliding right angle which moves along the stick. The measurement should be taken on the centre line of the body.

A long-bodied dog with well-laid-back shoulders and well-angulated hindquarters may appear to have a short coupling as the distance between the two parts is short in comparison with the body length. A good depth of body tends to give the appearance of short coupling, while the reverse is true of the shallow body. An obviously long-coupled dog often has upright shoulders, straight stifles and a shallow body.

We must also consider whether the dog is short in leg or long in body. If one were to shorten the legs of any specimen by, say, an inch (2.5cm), it would usually make the coupling appear longer because of the accentuation of the body length compared to the height.

All these features, however, are relative and can be judged in no other way than by comparison of one part against another and against an ideal representative of the breed, bearing in mind that each section is a component of the whole.

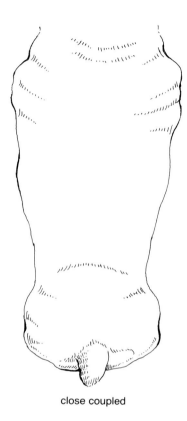

The couplings of an animal describe the section of the body from the last rib to the hip and give an indication of length of body. This drawing shows a close-coupled dog.

close coupled

Level topline   The Standard states 'level topline' with no further reference to the difference between what is regarded as the topline and what as the backline. Anatomically, the backline is represented by the six vertebrae of the thoracic spine directly behind the withers. For clarification purposes, we shall discuss the backline anatomically and refer to the entire length of the spinal column from withers to tail set-on as the topline of the dog.

The 'back' consists of the last six vertebrae, two bearing sternal ribs and the remaining four having asternal ribs, which are ribs not joined directly to the sternum and which seldom vary in length one from another. There can be no question that the power of the rear legs is delivered by thrust through the spine and consequently there is also no question of backline being anything but totally level and parallel with the ground when the dog is stationary with the spine straight.

79

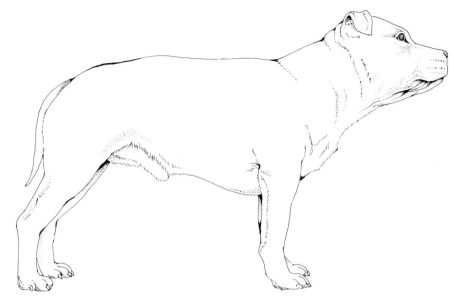

Drawing from photograph of a well-built and soundly constructed Staffordshire Bull Terrier.

Ch. Orchid Beauty. Note the level top from the withers to the hindquarters.

The topline, i.e. the entire length of the spinal column from forward of the withers to the tail set-on, should never be absolutely level, for the following reasons. The withers vertebrae differ from the rest in that they each have a long protruding spur which runs upwards at a backward inclined angle to provide support for the ligaments and muscles of the neck and scapulae. They are, therefore, higher than the rest of the topline of the dog.

A slight dip where the 'back' vertebrae meet the 'withers' vertebrae is usual and, unless severe, should not be faulted, since it would be almost impossible not to have a slight angle because of the change of direction of the spinal column between the end of the withers and the commencement of the back.

When moving, if the withers rise and fall to any marked degree, thereby disturbing the topline, the dog is spending his energy in lifting his centre of gravity when the action should in fact be propelling him along the line of travel, and this reduces the smoothness and efficiency of movement. When the dog is standing still this cannot be seen. Excessive rise and fall of the withers during movement is invariably indicative of bad conformation in the front and rear, which are not as well co-ordinated as they should be.

There should be a slight rise over the loin, as will be explained later in this section. From the back, the line will rise slightly over the loin and, as this breed has a sloping croup, the topline will then fall away to the tail. The spinal column is not rigid, and observation of the skeleton shows that the topline is not entirely even. The smooth appearance is the result of the development and shape of the back muscles. A topline that is entirely flat is usually lacking in flexibility.

Wide front and deep brisket These must be discussed together. Increasing the width and depth provides a greater capacity of the thorax and thus increased room for the heart and lungs. On the one hand, therefore, a deep body will normally allow greater endurance while a wide body has a centre of gravity so that the dog cannot easily be knocked off his feet.

The lungs lie one on each side of the thorax. Their external surfaces are curved and they fit snugly against the ribs. The internal surfaces meet to allow enough space for the passage of oesophagus, or gullet, leading to the stomach. The heart is suspended from approximately the mid-point of the thorax and lies centrally on the sternum between the third and eighth ribs.

81

Ch. Ashstock Max the Miller. Note the wide front and deep chest.

The expansion and contraction of the ribs, by increasing and decreasing the capacity of the thoracic cavity, aid respiration and provide a dog with the ability to obtain enough oxygen flow into the blood. The diaphragm muscle, which one can explain as a 'sheet' of muscle, extends from the loin vertebrae and travels diagonally forward, level with the seventh rib, and from there curves back a little to the rearmost end of the sternum to separate the thorax from the abdomen. This is one of the most important muscles and its main purpose is to aid breathing. As the muscle expands, it becomes flatter and creates a negative pressure on the faces of the lungs, which then expand to draw in air via the bronchial tubes. When it relaxes it returns to its curved shape and the used air is passed out of the lungs.

Well-sprung ribs The dog has thirteen pairs of ribs arising from the spine, nine of which are united below the sternum. The sternum or breast bone consists of bony sections firmly joined together. The first nine pairs of rib are joined to it by cartilages.

The rib is a highly elastic bone and has a head which articulates with the vertebrae. The eighth rib is usually the longest, while the other ribs are shorter in proportion so as to create the under curvature of the rib-cage. When the ribs move they rotate at the ball and socket joint of the head. When the lungs expand and air is inhaled, the rib rotates forward and, on exhalation of air, the ribs rotate back to their original portion.

The space between each rib is about twice the width of the adjacent rib, the space being filled by the intercostal muscle. This is a very important point since the wider the space between each rib the more thoracic capacity is obtained. The thorax is suspended by a sling of muscles between the scapulae and the arm bones.

One of the major muscles of the body is the great dorsal (thoracic) muscle (*latissimus dorsi*). Triangular in shape and broad, it begins over the loin and last four dorsal vertebrae, wraps around the rib-cage and terminates in a tendon inserted on the head of the humerus near the shoulder blade. It is this muscle which creates the ripples on the sides of the dog when moving.

Although the Standard calls for well-sprung ribs, and the capacity of the rib-cage is of utmost importance, the width must not exceed the width of the shoulder. In fact, it should extend only to just short of the width of the shoulder as can be seen in the illustration on page 79.

Ch. Truestaff Wild Orchid. Rather light in the loins; good topline.

Rather light in the loin   It is obvious the back legs of this dog are not designed to carry weight, as we shall discuss in the section on hindquarters. Considering this fact, we feel the Standard's instruction of 'rather light in the loin' is sensible.

The loins are carried on seven vertebrae which link the front and rear assemblies and have no other bony support. Lack of support is countered by the vertebrae arranged in a slight curve somewhat like the head of a bridge arch. The vertebra spines are inclined in a forward direction to support the rearing muscles which have a backward pull. Any sagging here, such as a sway back, would understandably be a serious structural fault. A slight rise over the loin is necessary although not indicated by the Standard.

A loin that is flat, and therefore lacking in flexibility, is undesirable and prevents total agility; this is a fact we have both observed in a bitch I owned. Her topline was very flat and it was possible to balance a cup upon it, which would not slide off during trotting movement. She was fast and never failed to run down a rabbit to bring home to her whelps (not allowed by me to her great disappointment) but fast as she was forward, she had enormous difficulty in climbing the rugged rocks and hills around our home. She certainly could not jump to any height and more often than not had to be given assistance by propping up her rear end to help her climb onto or over boulders in her path. If she happened to slide down a gully, she had difficulty in climbing back to the top. My other dogs were able to negotiate without problems the steep faces of the gully and any boulders in their way. I concluded that my bitch did not have the flexibility in the loin to perform with the agility required for this type of terrain.

Obviously then, there must be a slight rise over the loin to facilitate agility required in the hindquarters. You can use your own body as an example if you consider that your waist represents the coupling or loin of the dog. If you stand upright with knees locked and from that position jump forward you will find it necessary to bend the knees and waist to obtain the push off from the ground. Again, if you imitate the dog by using your arms as the forelegs, you will find that to move upward you must sink backward to transfer the centre of gravity to the rear and bend at the waist (which is the loin of the dog) to get off the ground.

A slight rise, however, must never be confused with camel or roach back, both of which are severe faults in conformation. The camel back arch arises as far forward as the withers, the roach back

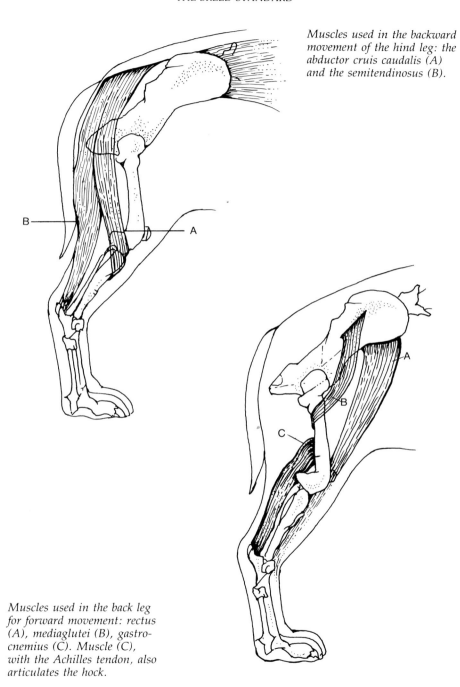

Muscles used in the backward movement of the hind leg: the abductor cruis caudalis (A) and the semitendinosus (B).

Muscles used in the back leg for forward movement: rectus (A), mediaglutei (B), gastro-cnemius (C). Muscle (C), with the Achilles tendon, also articulates the hock.

85

arises at about the twelfth vertebra and extends to the croup. With a croup that has a slight slope, the visual effect is obviously more pronounced. Both of these faults are severe in that the rear-end drive is transmitted through the spinal column and any excessive dip or rise in topline affects the forequarters' ability to sustain shock in landing, ability in jumping and the movement of the front legs.

A good tuck up of the loin is necessary since this is an area in which extra weight is not desired. The tuck should start at the ninth rib. If further forward, the thorax is being robbed of vital space and this becomes a fault in soundness. This is also the point where the rib-cage should be assessed and not at the point behind the elbows.

The Standard's instructions mean nothing, however, without due consideration of the entire spinal column which is very flexible and consists of a series of differently shaped strong bones called vertebrae. The spinal column runs from head to tail and holds the whole together so that the body literally hangs from the spine. Without a firm support for the spinal column there is no correct conformation. To maintain this alignment from neck to tail, the spine has numerous muscles, the most powerful being the long *issimus dorsi* which covers the entire length of the spinal column. The spinal column is not straight and has a series of essential gentle curves.

It is also well to remember the importance of good muscle. The skeleton is inanimate and cannot function without muscles. In this breed the muscles should be long and resilient and can be likened in quality to those of a boxer as opposed to a weight-lifter.

Hindquarters

UK and USA: The hindquarters should be well muscled, hocks let down with stifles well bent. Legs should be parallel when viewed from behind.

Whereas parts of the Standard make it difficult for faults in conformation not to be introduced, the hindquarter requirement is sound for our breed and, if attained, gives the animal the purpose and strength on the movement we desire.

The hindquarters are not designed to carry weight. The weight-bearing capacity between the front and back assemblies can easily be compared by gently pressing down on the withers and the rear which will show you that the front can sustain a great deal more

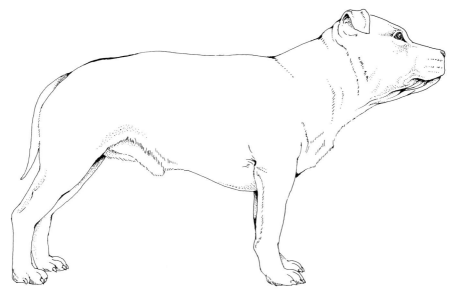

Level topline.

pressure than the rear. The back legs are required to impart power and thrust to the dog's movement and, moreover, power at whatever speed the animal needs to move, whether at a fast or slow gait. When stationary, the back legs are only supporting the rear body weight and thus the most efficient position for the legs is that they be vertical from the spinal column.

As with the Standard's lack of instruction on the degree of angulation of the scapulae and no instruction on an obviously necessary slight rise over the loin, there is also no instruction concerning the slope of the croup. However, the Standard calls for a 'low set-on tail' which, anatomically, can be obtained only by a steeper angulation of the croup and, therefore, the pelvis. We can then conclude that this breed has a sloping croup to the low tail set-on and must be judged accordingly.

The pelvis is attached to the three sacral vertebrae and it consists of three bones fused together on each side: the ilium, ischium and pubis. The ilium is the largest component. It is elongated in shape and is somewhat flattened and forms that portion of the pelvis in front of the hip joint. The ischium forms the posterior portion and the two join the pubis. Between the ischium and pubis is the

Rear legs must *be parallel.*
Hocks that turn in (cow hocks)
or that turn out (pin-toes) are
serious structural faults.

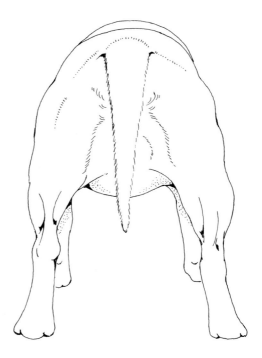

obturator foramen, a large opening to facilitate passage of blood vessels and nerves to the hind limbs. The upper end of the ilium articulates with the sacrum which forms the roof of the pelvic girdle.

The diameter of the pelvis is greater behind than in front. Facing the outer aspect of the floor of the pelvis is the acetabulum, the socket which houses the head of the femur to form a ball and socket joint, known as the hip joint. The acetabulum contains a notch open at the lower front end which provides attachment to the round ligament (teres ligament) which holds the head of the femur in the socket. If the head of the femur and the acetabulum do not fit together correctly, the ball loses its circular shape. It appears, from our research of statistics, that this breed is not prone to hip dysplasia and the percentage of incidence of this condition is very low.

The femur is a long, narrow, tubular and slightly curved bone with the great trochanter at the upper end near the head which provides attachment for the muscles. The 'well muscled' hindquarters instruction of the Standard can be seen in the strong pelvic muscles which assist in holding the parts of the hip joint together and control the movement of the head of the femur within the hip joint. The slope of the pelvis has a direct bearing on the hind legs and is the reason for the reduced length of rear stride, which is as well since the front leg movement in this breed precludes a long rear stride. The Standard calls for a 'well bent' stifle and we must, therefore, have a slope to the croup since a flat croup with a bent stifle would put more strain on the patella mechanism and the hip assembly during forward movement.

The well bent stifle requires longer tibia and fibula bones which extend to the hock joint, providing a long achilles tendon and muscles activating the joint. With the construction of the hind legs of this breed, we can well afford the short, well let down hock which must be straight and strong. The tibia and fibula articulate together at the upper end of the space between them, held together at both ends by fibrous ligaments. The tibia and fibula and the bones of the hock, with the metacarpals, make the hock joint, which carries seven bones with varying degrees of movement between them.

In our opinion, far too much emphasis is placed on the well bent stifle in this breed. It has been our experience that dogs with straight stifles are also extremely agile but the agility is commensurate with the purpose of the design of the dog.

Angulation of the stifle implies a flexed hip and stifle with extra length of the second thigh and shortened hock, which is called for in our Standard. However, if the bend of stifle is excessive and exaggerated the foot is then placed behind a vertical line from the seat bone of the pelvis (*tuber ischii*) to the ground instead of directly under the hip vertically from the spinal column, which is important for support of body weight.

In moving, the force obtained from pressure of the hind foot against the ground is transmitted to the pelvis and involves no wastage of power. There is a ligamental attachment between the pelvis and the sacrum, unlike the foreleg which is attached to the spine by musculation only. In the over-angulated stifle, the angle at which the tibia connects to the lower end of the fibula obstructs the correct and efficient drive. The quadriceps muscles extend the stifle joint and the tibia and fibia lock together only in extension. A well bent stifle is one thing, but an overly bent stifle is another and is indicative of trouble ahead for future generations. Moderation must be the operative answer to avoid this trend.

The centre of gravity is well forward in the Staffordshire Bull Terrier, and a slope to the pelvis, coupled with the very strong muscles, compensates to a degree for the front which has difficulty in supporting the centre of gravity. The sloping croup enables the dog to get the feet under the body, turn quickly and then put the strong muscles into action, allowing the feet to act as a pivot. This draws the weight to the rear and provides a more vigorous thrust forward toward its target. Owners of this breed are probably more aware of this attribute than of any other.

The patella is small and mostly contained in the *rectus femoris* muscle of the femur in front of the stifle joint, moving up and down within the trochlea groove. The medial patella groove has a lower lip than the outer. If the dog is 'bandy', i.e. stifle out, hock in (cow hock), medial laxation of the patella occurs. Anterior posterior conformation is more important in patella movement because the point of origin of the quadriceps group to the insertion in patella ligament will vary in accordance to the degree of this fault.

The conformation of the hindquarter region of the Staffordshire Bull Terrier, as specified in the Standard, provides the breed with the great and desired ability it has to jump from a static position, as well as turning and rearing at great speed in any direction, all essential attributes of the breed.

In our opinion it is impossible to overemphasize the importance of correct movement, and the knowledge to be able to assess it. We consider that the movement directive in the amended Standard, though helpful, describes the correct movement of any terrier breed and does not attempt to recognize the idiosyncracies of movement peculiar to our breed, which we have attempted to explain more fully in the section on movement.

Feet

UK: The feet should be well padded, strong and of medium size.
USA: The feet should be well padded, strong and of medium size. Dewclaws, if any, on the hind legs are generally removed. Dewclaws on the forelegs may be removed.

The Standard gives little instruction on the type of foot required in the Staffordshire Bull Terrier other than well padded and strong, and we would think this to be a normal requirement in any dog. Description of the feet is left as 'medium size'.

Generally, the foot considered to be the most desirable is the cat foot and the only other type categorized is the hare foot which

Irish Ch. Triple Crown of Tridwr. Note the correct tight feet.

probably gives greater leverage and speed but is not as efficient as the cat foot for endurance. In our opinion, there are two further types – the flat foot and splayed foot – all too often seen in our breed, both being undesirable and unsound.

The feet are designed to bear the entire weight of the dog, act as a brake to the limbs and are responsible for supporting the action of movement. As with us, sore or injured feet greatly hinder the mode of locomotion, as well as, we might add, affecting temperament! Flat and splayed feet are more often than not caused by lack of good exercise and diet.

An intricate construction of muscles, tendons, bones and ligaments control the foot and its shape. Terrier breeds generally desire the cat foot in which the toes are close together and arched at the joints, giving good angulation. In the hare foot, by a slight slackening of ligaments, the terminal joints are less angulated and the phalanges, therefore, lengthened. It is quite difficult sometimes to see much difference in the hare foot and the flat foot. The splayed foot gives little lift or support and is generally accompanied by weak pasterns. Muscles become stronger if the dog is properly exercised. Rough and hard terrain greatly assist in maintaining the well-arched foot while exercise on smooth or soft ground makes it easy for a flat foot to travel comfortably.

Therefore, the development of the feet is dependent upon the exercising surface, particularly in puppyhood. Poor feet might not always be due to faulty breeding or conformation, but to incorrect and limited exercise. Maintenance of pastern strength also relies on regular and correct exercise.

The pad on the forelimbs at the rear of the carpal bones of the knee is believed to be used as a brake pad in some breeds. As far as we can ascertain, it has no effect on the movement of our breed.

There are five digits to the foot. The first, on the inner side, is very small and is the dewclaw, allowed under USA Standard to be removed. We strongly endorse the removal of these digits within a few days of birth when it is painless and easy to accomplish. If left, they become a nuisance factor in easily being caught in long grasses or torn on rough terrain. To remove them in adulthood requires surgery and discomfort for the dog.

The dewclaw has only two phalanges and the remaining four toes have three each, the terminal phalange being quite small with a collar of bone at its base. A pad is attached beneath the end joint of each toe. A fifth pad, large and triangular in shape, sits in the centre hollow of the four digits and it is important that this pad is thick and sufficiently well developed to absorb the shock in forward movement. It also partly controls the downward angle of the toes, enabling the nails to wear through friction with the ground. If the pad is too thick, the toes point more upward and the nails then avoid friction contact and will grow and constantly require clipping. In the dewclaw, which never has any contact with the ground, the nail can grow without interference, often curling inward and penetrating the pad.

The hind feet are slightly smaller. It is equally essential that these pads and toes are well developed to enable the animal efficiently to transit the great muscular strength of the hindquarters into movement.

Tail

UK: The tail should be of medium length, low set, tapering to a point and carried rather low. It should not curl much, and may be likened to an old-fashioned pump handle.
USA: The tail is undocked, of medium length, low set, tapering to a point and carried rather low. It should not curl much and may be likened to the old-fashioned pump handle.
A tail that is too long or badly curled is a fault.

The USA Standard includes 'the tail is undocked' as a precaution to deter starting a fashion not conducive to the universal Standard. It also faults a too long or badly curled tail.

The tail is part of the spinal column and a short back is invariably followed by a short tail. We consider the clause 'of medium length' to be ambiguous and open to interpretation. Generally, it has been accepted that the tail should not extend below the point of the hock. Medium is defined as 'that which lies in the middle' therefore, 'of medium length' means the tail should be half of the length of a measurement from set-on to the ground.

If you measure from set-on to the near foot ground level in the picture of our model, you will find his tail to be a fraction longer than medium and, if extended to the hock, which is normally used as a guide to length, it would certainly not be of medium length. It would only meet the point of the hock if the dog's tail had a more pronounced curve to extend the length in measuring, which it does not have and should not have. With the short hock of this breed, measuring to the hock joint for medium length is, therefore, incorrect but we concede it is a useful guide.

The low set of the tail has already been discussed since it has such a bearing on the slope of the croup. The instruction of the Standard that it should not curl much, and may be likened to an 'old-fashioned pump handle' is a poor instruction since, in actual fact, it should not curl at all if likened to the old-fashioned pump handle which had a slight curve and not a curl. However, again, we concede this to be a fair guide, providing one is acquainted with an old-fashioned pump handle.

A normal tail, without the kinks and knots that are seen occasionally, is an indication of the construction of the entire spinal column and, therefore, an important part of the body. There are two muscles that activate the tail: at the set-on and at the terminal point.

The two set-on muscles (lateralis) are the continuation of the muscles used to tense the loin and arise from behind the rib-cage. If the tail is curled it generally indicates loss of tension in the terminal muscle. A corkscrew or pig-tail that sometimes happens in our breed may be caused by lack of tension in one of the lateralis muscles at the set-on. The coccygeal vertebrae of the tail begin behind the last sacral vertebrae where the pelvis attaches to the spinal column. Two or three vertebrae are present between the sacral vertebrae and the set-on of the tail, but cannot be seen. If the tail tapers smoothly to a point and shows no sign of knots or kinks, it is giving a clear indication of the good condition of the entire spinal column.

The tail is not an inanimate part of the body, and carriage of the tail certainly indicates the health and mental attitude of the dog. If observed well, your dog will tell you how he is feeling by his tail carriage.

There are various expressions to describe tail faults – ring, hook, gay, pig, etc. – but really it matters little what they are called. Breeders and fanciers need only to know when they have the correct tail, how to maintain it in future generations and realize that the set of the tail indicates whether the spinal column is correct, strong and healthy.

Height and Weight

UK and USA: Weight: Dogs: 28 to 38 pounds.
Bitches: 24 to 34 pounds.
Height at shoulder: 14in to 16in, these heights being related to weight. Non-conformity with these limits is a fault.

The Standard is explicit in its instruction but totally inexplicable in reason and intent. Let us first break down the height to weight clause of the Standard.

Dogs   14in – 28lb = 2lb per 1in
15in – 33lb = 2lb per 1in for 14in and 5lb per additional 1in
16in – 38lb = 2lb per 1in for 14in and 10lb per additional 2in

therefore:

14in – 28lb = 2lb per 1in
15in – 33lb = 2lb 3oz (approx.) per 1in
16in – 38lb = 2lb 6oz per 1in

Bitches   14in – 24lb = 1lb 11oz per 1in (approx.)
15in – 29lb = 1lb 11oz per 1in and 5lb per additional 1in
16in – 34lb = 1lb 11oz per 1in and 10lb per additional 2in

therefore:

14in – 24lb = 1lb 11oz per 1in
15in – 33lb = 1lb 15oz per 1in
16in – 34lb = 2lb 2oz per 1in

Under this directive it is highly doubtful whether eye evaluation can correctly determine that a 15½in dog weighs 35½lb. If we are serious in complying with the Standard, why then do we not insist on weight and measure tests prior to entering the show ring? We venture to suggest the result would be a ring devoid of exhibits!

The ratio requires an increase in weight for a dog over 14in at 5lb per 1in as it does for the bitches, but they fare less well since they share the same ratio, and carry the same height clause as the dog but with an initial 4lb loss of weight to height. Where is all this sudden increase in weight lodged? In the bitches it would be possible in advanced pregnancy or when there is a large litter of whelps to feed and she is endowed with the necessary equipment!

The penalty for non-conformation in height and weight is only a single fault and judges would, therefore, be within their right to put up a 17in, 43lb dog if, in their opinion, it is the only fault the dog carried against other exhibits with more faults. Do not think this cannot happen – it already has and effectively wipes out the possible intent of the Standard.

According to the structure indicated in the Standard, the Staffordshire Bull Terrier is a positive animal. An inch is a very small measure to carry the additional 5lb in weight and, therefore, the 16in dog with the extra 10lb is more visually exciting and positive example of the breed than a 14in dog. The Standard is, then, guilty

Ch. Kerrisdale Orchid's Fancy and Orchid Firefly. Neither conformed to the Standard directive regarding height to weight ratio.

of preference in size and appears to us to disfavour the smaller animal allowed under the Standard.

The bitch is required to comply in all respects to the directive of acquiring the same anatomical structure and desired features yet is denied the same weight to height ratio. In fact, the bitch carries a penalty in the initial reduction of weight to height. Nowhere does the Standard indicate that bitches should be different in conformation. General appearance clearly states: 'the Staffordshire Bull Terrier should be of great strength for its size and although muscular, should be active and agile'. It does not indicate bitches should be anything less, yet denies them, through the weight and height clause, even competition with the dog. It is no wonder that there are so few Best of Breed bitches.

If the bitch does attain the same weight as the dog, she is, more often than not, described as a 'doggy' bitch but there is no such thing, particularly under this Standard. She can be referred to as overweight, overdone or too bulky but not 'doggy'.

In the wild community of the canine family, the work load for survival is the same for both sexes. In fact, the bitch carries an extra burden when producing and rearing her young. Mother Nature does not penalize the bitch with restrictions on her ability to survive by a reduced weight to height ratio, nor does she require the bitch to have a different appearance from that of the dog. The word 'dog' and 'bitch' are words to differentiate the sex, not outward build or ability. The fact that we have a domesticated animal does not mean the bitch should be less rugged, strong, capable or different in outward typical appearance from the male.

Under the Breed Standard, in the final judging for Best of Breed, the judge's decision must, therefore, be based upon, 'is this a better bitch than this is a dog?' when it should be 'which is the best representative of the breed?'. From experience, it will rarely be the bitch under this Standard, a regrettable fact since the quality of the bitches is the foundation of the breed. In our opinion, a good dog is certainly worth his weight in gold, but a good bitch is priceless. The Standard, by its division of height and weight is forcing the separation of sexes to the disadvantage of the bitch.

We cannot conceive the rationale behind the Standard's unrealistic height to weight ratio which, to our knowledge, is well ignored. Nonconformity carries a fault and not a disqualification. Therefore, if this directive was meant to control the size of the exhibit, it cancels its intent by lack of penalty substance and lack of a requirement for a weight and measure test prior to acceptance in the show ring. In our opinion, there should be a restrictive maximum height clause of 16in with no weight ratio since the Standard dictates the desired construction for balanced conformation and *type* cannot be attained under this ratio of height to weight.

Coat

UK: Smooth, short and close to the skin.
USA: Smooth, short and close to the skin, not to be trimmed or dewhiskered.

Very little comment is needed in this clause which has been interpreted well by fanciers, although 'short' perhaps is a little ambiguous, as is 'close to the skin' since the coat grows from the skin. Possibly, 'short, smooth and dense' would have been a better description.

Added to the USA Standard is 'not to be trimmed or dewhiskered'. This was specially included to ensure a natural dog and as a deterrent to the practice of tail trimming, normal in the UK. The Staffordshire Bull Terrier is a rugged and individual animal and it was believed the tail should reflect this as part of the whole dog, particularly in the maintenance of overall balance. It was decided that a line-up of dogs all with trimmed tails looking identical and created to acquire neatness, would spoil and change the rugged character and if such a tail was desired, it should be bred. In other words, the dog should look as though he owns his tail and it is not man-made.

Coat Colour

UK and USA: Red, fawn, white, black or blues, or any of these colours with white. Any shade of brindle or any shade of brindle with white.
UK: Black-and-Tan or Liver colour not to be encouraged.
USA: Black-and-Tan or Liver colour to be disqualified.

Does the Standard mean *one* of these colours with white, or *more* than one of these colours together with white? Is it meant to be singular or plural? It is important to the interpretation. If singular, any one colour with white means a single colour with white marking. The white dog must, therefore, be entirely white. If 'any of these colours' is plural, as in a red dog that has a black foreface (mask) and black on the tail, why then is the black-and-tan not accepted, particularly with white marking. The Standard gives no instruction as to how much black and tan is allowable, if any.

How do we deal with the directive of 'black-and-tan or liver colour not to be encouraged' in the UK Standard? The instruction is negative and carries no penalty as in the USA Standard. There is, therefore, no obstruction under the UK Standard to compete in the show ring with a black-and-tan or liver coloured dog and expect to be properly judged. Judges would be within their right to accept them in the ring and give honours to such a dog, rightly defending the action by stating, after fully taking into account that the colour is not to be encouraged, that it is the best specimen under the requirements of the Breed Standard. At the same time he could well dismiss white dogs with colour markings since they are not a defined colour in the Standard.

It must be remembered that although the Standard, at best, is only a guide, it is, however, the Bible of the Breed and if it has a directive to give, it should be given in clear and concise language, leaving no doubt as to its intent, particularly so where undesirable features should have a penalty clause. It may have been understandable when the breed was in its show infancy and the number of exhibits very limited. Now, however, with the Staffordshire Bull Terrier being one of the most populous of all Terrier breeds (in the UK), there is no longer a need to make any concession for animals whose colour is deemed undesirable. It is also significant that the percentage of breeder judges is extremely high in the UK and far less in other countries, particularly the USA, where judges must rely upon the wording of the Standard.

Black-and-Tan or liver colour cannot be entered in the AKC show ring since they are penalized with a clear disqualification. Even so, there has been a great deal of argument that, with white markings, the black-and-tan is then tri-colour, and such an animal was accepted into the show ring, presumably as a tri-colour since 'with or without white' was not clearly stated in the disqualification penalty.

Genetics of Coat Colour   The study of colour genetics is vast and abstruse, needing a full programme of experimental breedings with a great deal of study of genetic colour code. Colour genes carried by the individual dog are not visibly apparent and can only be discovered with intense study, starting with the chromosomes and ending with matings that produce whelps of a known and forecastable colour from each animal. This would be impossible with bitches because of the restriction of the number of offspring she could produce. (If we were fanciers of the *Drosophila melanogaster* (fruit fly) it would be simple since the life cycle is 10–15 days and the females produce a hundred or more offsprings!) Finally, if and when you had the answer to the genetic colour behaviour of your stud dog, it would have been an exercise in futility in that by then he probably would be too old to stand on his feet let alone perform a mating service in the cause of scientific fact.

We have diligently studied and read various excellent books on this subject but have found that opinions differ. If our breed had evolved with one colour, it would be beneficial to maintenance of colour or colours to study the genetic make-up of the colour code. The late Mr Beilby made a heroic attempt to educate us by his book, but it was much too simplistic to be of any real general use. Each dog determines the coat colour it can transmit to its offsprings by action of at least ten different genes or gene pairs.

It seems to us that a breed carrying a Standard which allows several colours, together or apart, gives us little chance of thorough exploration of colour genetics and at this time we do not have a particular breed problem on colour, and will not have, unless the percentage of the undesirable colours of liver and black-and-tan increases in number. We believe that a little knowledge is a dangerous thing and our limited understanding of colour genetics in this breed precludes any attempt to impart an opinion. We concede that any theory we might have would be information not scientifically or practically proven.

Movement

If a dog is properly constructed and in good health, an observer should be able to assess from his movement whether or not he is a good sound representative of the breed. There are many physical faults, both structural and muscular that can, to a large extent, be hidden or at least camouflaged by an efficient handler when the dog is expertly 'stacked' for the show ring. However, as soon as the dog becomes mobile, any faults in the exhibit's conformation will become apparent.

For instance, a specimen that is loose in the shoulder can be supported by his handler so expertly that while stationary he appears to be quite sound, but as soon as he starts to move and the shoulders rotate, the animal's elbows point out in the completion of each forward stride and any reasonably competent judge, even our ringside judges, would be well able to see this and penalize the dog accordingly. Couplings, topline, length and ranginess and many other imperfections of construction can more accurately be assessed when the animal is moving.

Most judges in the USA have the dogs moving around the perimeter of the ring to assess and compare movement of all exhibits in the class. This was also the procedure in the past in the UK but is used far less these days and it seems to us that the discontinuance of this part of the judging was a retrograde step.

In our opinion, it is impossible to overemphasize the importance of correct assessment of movement. It is also our opinion that although the Staffordshire Bull Terrier has no movement clause in the present Standard and, therefore, is without instruction on any idiosyncrasies of the breed movement, every breeder, exhibitor and judge who has a genuine desire to further the improvement of the breed will read and think about the following observations. We do not claim that our conclusions are totally irrefutable (although we are confident they are correct), but in any event they will surely give a good basis for both consideration and discussion.

It is our opinion that the Staffordshire Bull Terrier movement is quite different from that of most, if not all, other terriers. However, if the specimen is soundly constructed and well conditioned, the basic movement is one that is correct for a dog, allowing for variations in movement imposed by the physical construction of this breed and unlike that of a terrier, even our close cousin the Bull Terrier.

As with all sound dogs, when a Staffordshire Bull Terrier is moving at the pace required in the show ring, i.e. a fast walk or a collected trot, the rear legs give the impression of supplying great power and drive while the forelegs reach out well in front in order to give the rear legs scope and room to express power visibly. Also ideally, they should move 'square' at both fore and rear ends, without tending to move the feet in towards the centre of the line of travel as many exhibits seem to do.

The movement of our model has been recognized as first class by knowledgeable students of this breed. Indeed, Mr Arthur Taylor of Australia, International All-Round judge and Staffordshire Bull Terrier breeder and specialist, when judging our model described his movement as, 'the best Staffordshire Bull Terrier movement I have ever seen from any dog of this breed, at any time and at any place. This dog's movement is superb and wholly typical for this breed.'

We realized that in trying to assess our model's movement, the eye cannot possibly record it in detail, step by step, and if we wished to examine closely a complete cycle of movement, we would have to obtain the movement photographed clearly and in great detail. This was easier said than done. We needed still pictures of the movement. We tried through video and movies but neither were satisfactory as the stills did not give us the clarity of details we required.

After many months of failing in our endeavour we began to lose hope of being able to produce anything more accurate and factual than the line-drawings of movement used in many books, which really must only be illustrations based on conjecture of perfect and desired movement. Finally, it was our great good fortune to obtain the expert help of photographer Mrs Stephen Dalton who, with a very fast camera, gave us the illustrations shown opposite to show, in detail, what we were looking for in the correct locomotion of the Staffordshire Bull Terrier.

We will discuss the movement first when viewed from the side. It will be noted that we have printed two 'five-pace sequences', the second set to confirm the action of the first. The background will more easily enable the reader to follow the forward sequences.

(a)   The subject has begun moving and it will be seen that the left rear leg has been used to give impetus to moving the body, with the left foreleg and right rear leg bearing the body weight. During this action the right foreleg is making no contact with the ground but is about to be placed firmly to carry the weight of the forequarters. Obviously, at this moment of transference of balance from left to right sides, there is going to be a slight swing of the body, particularly so in that the breed has a very wide front with comparative lightness of the rear assembly and a centre of balance well forward of that of most terrier breeds.

(b)   The right forefoot has been firmly placed and, although the left rear leg is also in contact with the ground, it is well to the rear and in that position can have no great significance as a weight-bearing limb. It is in this position that weakness and looseness of the shoulder would become apparent in that the scapula would be inclined inward and the elbow visibly turned outward. An indication of the weight being sustained by the foreleg will be realized if one studies the great amount of bend there is in the pastern angulation.

The left foreleg is at its maximum forward reach and is, to us, one of the most surprising aspects of the movement. We had not expected or thought that a typical Staffordshire Bull Terrier carrying a heavy rib-cage, coupled with lack of scapula angulation, would be able to 'throw' the foreleg so far forward yet still retain straightness in the required limb's movement.

(c)   The dog is now well into his stride. The right hind leg has been placed down and its thrust has carried the body over the right

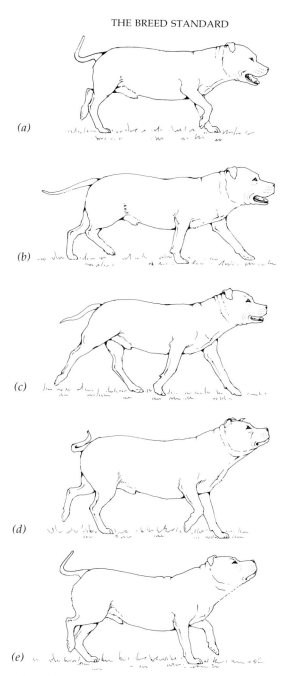

(a)

(b)

(c)

(d)

(e)

These drawings have been made from movement photographs and illustrate the complete cycle of movement.

103

foreleg, which has swung well forward to the full extent of its reach. The left rear leg is well forward and just coming into contact with the ground. At this moment it seems to be bearing no weight and for a split second the entire body is practically 'airborne', as very definitely only the toes of the left foreleg are making contact with the ground. Also, take note that in this brief second the dog appears to be pacing, although he definitely did not pace during the cycle of movement.

We feel it well to point out that the position of the head has lifted very slightly during the period of movement and accentuated considerably during the last two pictures. This had to be due to his arrival at the end of his short walk, doubtless looking for reward from his mistress.

Interesting to us is the subject's topline which, very steady and ideally level in the first three illustrations, begins to show a slight dip at the withers in (d), increasing greatly when he lifts his head very high in (e).

(d)   The right rear leg and left foreleg have travelled into a similar position to (a). The dog is now in the full momentum of his movement and these members are again bearing the body weight. The left rear leg is preparing to swing forward and to be placed down to start the sequence again.

(e)   It will be seen that, having completed one cycle of movement, the limbs are again in a very similar position to (b). In reality, this bridges a split second of time between the static positions of (a) and (b) but with a very apparent difference in the head position which has lifted considerably with consequent deterioration of the topline. It should be noted that the tail position has reverted to a similar one to (a). Obviously, this is an aid to balance in the continuation of movement.

Forward Front Movement

(a)   The dog is already in motion and it will be noted that the entire body weight is being sustained on the left foreleg and is square to the shoulder, with no looseness. Obviously, the right foreleg is at forward reach and, although it is difficult to determine accurately, it appears that the left rear leg is practically in its forward position waiting its turn to sustain body weight.

(b)   The body has swung slightly to the right. The right foreleg is in the rear position of movement and the left foreleg is, at this

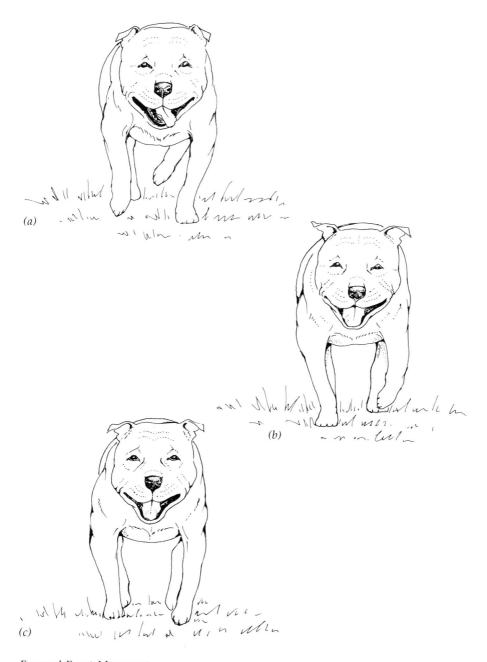

(a)

(b)

(c)

Forward Front Movement

moment, about to be placed on the ground, while the left rear leg has completed its push and moved to the rear.

(c)   Here the right foreleg and left rear leg are bearing the weight of the body. At this moment the body has completed a slight movement to the right and is quite clearly showing the side of the dog. The left foreleg and right rear leg are clear of the ground, and it should be noted that with the dog in this position, a weight transference is about to be made to the opposite side. There is already in this picture a slight leaning to the left, illustrated by the fact that the body weight is slightly over the left foreleg.

Rear Action

Only two figures are suitable to discuss the movement with which the dog goes away from the observer (*see* illustrations on page 107). They show quite clearly the two aspects of movement we think important. The first, seen in both illustrations, is that the limbs move 'square' i.e. straight from hip to stifle to hock to foot and from shoulder to pastern as they should, and our model lifts his legs high enough (in (a) right rear and left foreleg) to show the pads clearly. It is most interesting to note that as the legs swing straight, the body definitely tends to lean to the side where the foreleg is taking the weight of the dog. We conclude that this gives the Staffordshire Bull Terrier that rather specialized but very typical movement which in our opinion is often wrongly criticized by non-specialist judges.

Any animal will, within the limit of its construction, use the easiest and most economical pace it can to move at the speed it requires at any particular moment, and it appears to us that the body swing of the Staffordshire Bull Terrier demonstrates this.

   In our opinion, any deviation from 'straightness' in movement is invariably caused by some peculiarity or fault in construction. To demonstrate this, a dog whose legs are too short for his height invariably moves 'close' both front and rear. When stationary, it tends to place the legs, and in particular the forelegs, in towards the body centre.

   The Staffordshire Bull Terrier should – and a sound specimen does – move with great purpose, and it is because of the greater width of the front in comparison with the rear that we have a swing of the body towards the weight-bearing side. In other words,

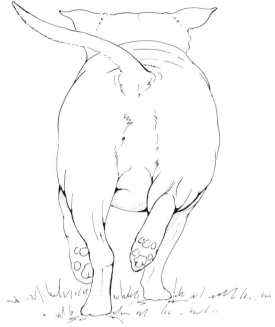

The right rear leg swinging to the centre of the body confirms the aspect of movement shown in (a) on page 105.

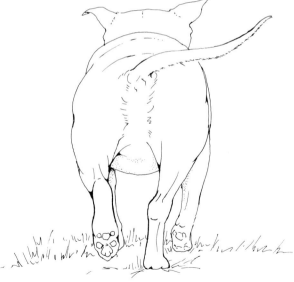

Here, weight and balance is transferring to the left.

107

because of *soundness* of movement, the rear legs, while giving push and purpose to the movement, swing over slightly to the opposite diagonal in order to push the body along in the most efficient way and maintain balance with momentum. One must always bear in mind that a correctly constructed limb is articulated by well-developed and efficient musculation designed to move 'straight' and cannot do otherwise without strain on both muscle and joint.

There is no mention of a sway or roll, as we refer to it, in the Standard and this appears to be one of the major problems to non-specialist judges. The roll of the Staffordshire Bull Terrier should not be confused with the roll of the Bulldog which emanates from behind the shoulder. The Staffordshire Bull Terrier, particularly when slow-trotting, is extremely light and bouncy on his feet, almost as though he possesses rubber feet pads. The Standard of construction requires a great width of front assembly and a well-developed rib-cage, with lightness in the loins and lesser width in the rear, and it must, therefore, be obvious that with the transference of weight in movement, particularly as the centre of gravity (which incidentally, we have measured) is well forward to approximately the fourth or fifth rib, the dog must sway or roll. The lightness of foot and the bouncing action accentuates this movement.

A good number of Staffordshire Bull Terriers pace on occasions. This is unacceptable to most Terrier Judges and a reason to leave the dog out of the winning line-up. We have heard many theories on why the dog paces: overweight, tired, of poor construction, among other reasons. It has been our experience that the Staffordshire Bull Terrier does not pace under any of these conditions. In fact, it is rather the opposite.

From our observation, pacing appears when the dog is fit, well conditioned and extremely excited or happy. Our model enjoyed the show ring, was happy, excited and attacked the procedure with great gusto. On entering the ring with great animation, he invariably proceeded to pace his way to his place in the ring. It required a good speed to avoid this initial 'happy' pacing. Under normal everyday conditions he did not pace at all.

A superbly moving bitch one of the authors owned in California would win the top honour time and again over other equally excellent specimens by virtue of her movement, yet when exuberant, particularly at free exercise time, she paced at great speed. She certainly was not tired and exhibited great excitement and joy at the prospect of her daily exercise. Her companion bitch was well built and although, in spite of every effort she was always overweight, at no time did she pace. We discussed at length the question of pacing during our conversations with Professor Clayton-Jones who could give us no anatomical reasons for pacing or why it should be considered as anything other than a natural action of choice by individual animals.

If a dog is pacing, the judge should indicate this to the exhibitor and allow a change of speed of locomotion. It is our opinion, and we believe that of most good judges, that pacing is not indicative of unsound construction. Since there is no instruction on movement in the Standard of the breed, each individual judge and breeder has assessed movement according to personal conception of what is correct. Therefore, there are going to be variations in movement. It is our hope that through these pictures the mystery of the movement of this breed will be more fully understood.

Type or Soundness

Time and again the question of judging for type or soundess is discussed. By the use of the word 'or' the words 'type' and 'soundness' become opposites, thereby making one quality more important than the other. There are many knowledgeable people who insist that type must be the most important, using the example that a mongrel can be extremely sound but lack type. Does it lack type? The mongrel is a member of the species *Canis Familiaris* (domestic dog), sub-species Mongrel and, therefore, has classification as a type of dog. The difference is the lack of breeding to precise conformation under a Breed Standard carrying known Pedigree for many generations. A mongrel should be instantly recognized as such when viewed against a pure-bred dog that has been produced to a Standard of precise conformation. And, supposing one accepts the theory that a mongrel can be sound but not typical, is that a justified reason to believe that the Staffordshire Bull Terrier may be typical but unsound?

Type can be defined as the physical make-up of the dog which enables us instantly to recognize him as being a pure-bred representative of a particular breed. Soundness simply means that an animal has all its proper mental and physical parts, making a typical example of the breed it represents in compliance with the

Ch. Rellim Taskforce of Nozac. A superb example of correct breed type.

Standard of the breed. For example, a Staffordshire Bull Terrier with prick ears as opposed to the Standard's required rose ears is not unsound but is untypical, but if the dog has the perfect rose ears required under the Standard but is deaf, it is typical but unsound since the hearing mechanism is not functioning properly.

Generally, when the soundness of a dog is discussed, it seems mainly to be focused on the obvious, i.e. the structure of the body. Indeed, the body must be sound but it should not be forgotten that soundness also incorporates temperament. A dog cannot be sound in body and not in temperament and be considered typical. Temperament is part of the soundness and possibly the greatest

110

attribute the Staffordshire Bull Terrier offers and which all too often is not given much consideration either in breeding programmes or judging in the show ring.

Temperament makes this proud, gentle, intelligent animal, coupled as it should be with superb athleticism and great joy of living, the enthusiastic and treasured family companion he is. Indeed, on first meeting a Staffordshire Bull Terrier, it is the temperament that impresses far more than anything else since he is not, to the uninitiated, a particularly handsome animal.

It is of utmost importance to remember that breeding for type without equal regard for soundness (which includes temperament) may be laying a foundation for later trouble and distress to owners, the majority of whom keep their dogs as pets rather than for exhibition. Unfortunately, in many instances, it takes time for unsoundness in a dog to become apparent and, if disregarded, this will cause serious problems in later generations.

The show ring is the shop-window of the breed, and it is obvious that judges, by their decisions, have a prime influence in retaining or losing type and soundness. Many an untypical and unsound dog has made its way to championship status due to judges who are less than competent in a breed, or with a mental bias for a specimen with a particular much-admired physical characteristic, at the expense of serious faults in type or soundness. Also, let us not forget, that by skilful handling and manoeuvring, exhibitors and handlers can knowingly be guilty of taking such specimens to the winner's corner.

Generally, winning dogs are sought after as breeding specimens, and it is absolutely essential that judges, breeders and exhibitors are responsible, competent, and fully realize the great responsibility they have that type, soundness and temperament must never be separated. If not, the tremendous and justified regard for this breed will disappear very quickly. Regarding this, the 1987 amendment to the Standard directs that, 'Male animals should have two apparently normal testicles descended into the scrotum.' This clause will obviously debar monorchids and chryptorchids, however good in other respects, from being awarded high placement in the show ring.

The New Standard

Recently, there has been a revision of the Breed Standard by The

111

Kennel Club in England. Most of the changes are of a minor nature and of little consequence.

One of the inclusions is an explanation of movement which calls for the dog to 'move with purpose', which is somewhat unnecessary since all dogs, if healthy, move with purpose dependent upon the reason he has for moving at any given time.

Changing wording in the Standard for clarification is one thing but changing the construction of the dog is another and will eventually create problems, take many generations to meet the requirement and will definitely affect the visual view of the dog, the weight clause and present-day movement. This has come about simply by the exclusion of 'rather light in the loins'.

It should not be taken lightly or overlooked by fanciers of this breed who believe the Staffordshire Bull Terrier is light in the loins now, has always been light in the loins and will continue to be 'light in the loins'. It should be remembered that the Breed Standard made the breed we have today and the revision will make it what it will be tomorrow. Under All-Round and Terrier judges, who are obliged to judge on the dictate of the Standard, the breed will change, however gradually.

By this deletion, fanciers and breeders must now accept a critical change in the anatomical construction and they will face a very long fight over many generations to make the change to comply with the Standard, since anatomical reconstruction cannot be achieved overnight.

The exclusion of this clause will also affect the weight clause by virtue of losing the lighter weight in the loin, and, for his height, the dog will carry more weight in that area, become 'cloddy' and thereby lose the required agility dictated by the Standard.

Hindquarters will be affected under the present Standard's instruction of 'well let down with stifles well bent'. Such construction would not be able to sustain the additional weight that will arise from the deletion of 'lightness in the loin'. It is possible the dog might be able to continue to be 'powerful' in movement but probably will not be able to sustain 'free' and 'agile'.

It must be remembered that each part of the anatomical construction must relate one part to the other and, if the breed is to survive as the popular breed it is now, second thought should be given to this change in the Standard. It appears to us that the change has been made without anatomical knowledge and forces a construction change of the breed without input from owners and breeders. This must be considered to be detrimental to the breed. The deletion has not been made from the American Kennel Club Standard and cannot be changed other than by a majority vote of members of Regional Clubs through the Parent Club.

3

Buying your Puppy or Dog

Why a Staffordshire Bull Terrier?

People who are not familiar with the Staffordshire Bull Terrier must, we are sure, sometimes wonder why so many seemingly intelligent owners are owned by one or more animals of this breed. The uninitiated will, and indeed do, point out with some justification that the breed is not at all distinguished in appearance, and 'lumpy' is sometimes the short description of the animal's physique. Among other complaints, they say the head is too big for the body. Some time ago a small boy was watching a lovely white bitch of mine exercising on Ham Common, chasing and returning to me a yellow ball. As she galloped back to me he remarked, 'Mister, that looks more like a pig with a lemon in its mouth than it does a dog!'

Why then do so many people, some of whom have many years' experience of other breeds, fall under the spell of the Staffordshire Bull Terrier, so much so that, in spite of its comparatively recent recognition as a pedigree breed, it is at this time the most popular and numerous of all terriers in the United Kingdom? Whether or not this is a good thing for the breed will always be of serious concern to those breeders who have the welfare and improvement of the breed as their aim, rather than a quick profit.

One of the main reasons for buying a pure-bred is that at least the prospective owner will know that the adult dog will be very much like the specimens he has seen. Some choose a dog they remember fondly from childhood, or on the recommendation of a friend or relative. However, there are many other considerations that should influence the choice. If the prospective owner gives thought to what he requires from a dog, he will, at least, consider the ability of that breed to fit in to the requirements and life-style of the owner.

Is there a garden? Is the owner an energetic type who likes walking and exercise? Will the dog be left alone during the day?

114

A white, bully-type bitch.

Does the owner wish the dog to participate in any sporting activities in which they may be interested and, very importantly, can he offer the dog an environment in which he can live as naturally as possible within the restrictions imposed by our modern civilization?

115

Castlebanks Bomber, who stood 17in at the shoulder and weighed 39lb.

As we have explained, most, if not all breeds, were originally conceived for some specific purpose. Therefore, by virtue of the ingrained hereditary instincts that have been bred in a specific breed for many generations, when placed in an environment completely foreign to these natural instincts, there could be some rebellion from the dog when he reaches maturity.

Obviously, a large breed is going to be more expensive to keep and will need a great deal of exercise, whereas a smaller breed would be a much better choice if the area in which the owner lives does not offer an opportunity for the dog to exercise sufficiently. Should you live in a rural area, you must be able to control the animal at all times. The responsibility for your dog's behaviour is yours and a free-running uncontrolled country dog will, through his actions, involve his owner in problems and perhaps heavy costs.

A total devotee of one breed is certainly going to be very prejudiced in favour of this breed and it would not be very sensible to consult such a person. Do remember, when you buy a dog, that the choice is yours and, if your choice is wrong, the fault lies with you and not the dog. His only desire will be to become a part of your family and please you.

Under normal circumstances you are buying a creature that will be with you for anything from ten to fifteen or more years and you should realize this and be prepared to accept the responsibilities of being the owner. You will have to train the dog, protect him and be responsible for him and his actions. In return he will doubtless be a source of joy to you and your family, guard and care for you to the best of his ability and, in terms of pleasure and affection, will contribute to the quality of your life.

We know, by the fact that you have taken the trouble to obtain and hopefully read this book, that you are seriously considering the breed type of dog known as the Staffordshire Bull Terrier. He is a dog of medium size, short coated and whose temperament and intelligence is such that, if well cared for, he is able to live in either town or country and has the capacity to be a more than satisfactory companion. He has a great affection for children, having earned the title of 'nursemaid dog' many years ago. He is easy to train, providing the owner is willing to take the time to teach him.

There have been many Staffordshire Bull Terriers trained to excel in obedience, entitling them to the honour of 'Companion Dog Excellent'. Many years ago Captain Warwick of Canterbury had two Staffordshire Bull Terriers who were accorded this honour. One of

Bedgbury Chieftan C.d.ex. stood 18in at the shoulder and weighed 47lb. He held the record for jumping length.

of them, known as Bedgbury Chieftain, was exhibited in fêtes and shows throughout the southern counties area and, by virtue of these exhibitions, was able to perform with great success and did a great deal to popularize the Staffordshire Bull Terrier in the early post-war years. He was a fine specimen but, even for those days, was too big to be exhibited in the show ring. However, his extra size, allied with a superb physique, enabled him to compete very successfully with other breeds entered in trials that had been the

118

province of the German Shepherd Dog. Capt. Warwick, an ex-Royal Marine, assured me that he had never found the need to chastise physically any of his dogs at any time. If treated with kindness and patience he believed the average Staffordshire Bull Terrier would respond with everything of which he is capable.

Both authors are, of course, very enthusiastic owners and breeders of the Staffordshire Bull Terrier. Possibly our opinion of dogs is rather biased in favour of this breed, which we have both owned and shown for well over forty years. However, we have had experience of living with various other breeds, mainly Fox Terriers, Airedales and German Shepherds. We have concluded that we like all dogs but have decided that the Staffordshire Bull Terrier is the most satisfying house dog and companion.

Finding your Staffordshire Bull Terrier

Do you want to own a dog to show or breed from, or just as a family pet? In any event, by far the wisest course is to go to a few dog shows at which Staffordshire Bull Terriers will be on view and have a good look at the animals being shown, noting their behaviour and attitude. Talk to as many owners and breeders as you can. You will find that, by and large, owners of our breed are one of the friendliest sections of the canine fraternity and will willingly give you opinions of their own stock and, of course, such is the nature of the dog breeder, doubtless give you an opinion of other breeders' stock! Therefore, you must talk with and listen to as many owners as you possibly can and then make your assessment of the breed from what you have heard and seen. As a spectator you are bound to form your own conclusions and prefer some stock on view to other exhibits.

You will find that the stock of all top breeders is stable. This means that although some breeders are obviously producing good all-round quality, they do have preferences for some particular aspect of the animals they produce. Generally it is the head of the dog that many breeders are very particular about and we have, in Chapter 2, tried to illustrate how very difficult it is to produce consistently the required head shape. Many breeders whose opinions have great validity consider that over the years there has been far too much emphasis on the production of this aspect of the dog to the degree that we are now in danger of losing the symmetry

Bearcats Bellamour, one of the first home-bred winners in the USA. Bred by Steve Stone. Owned by Lilian Rant.

and balance that is such an essential part of the physical make-up of the breed.

Many areas in the USA have banned the ownership of the Pitbull Terrier and, unfortunately, through lack of knowledge of dog breeds, included the American Staffordshire Terrier, the Staffordshire Bull Terrier and the Bull Terrier. All three breeds are registered by the American Kennel Club and none is used for pit-fighting. The American Kennel Club has, indeed, made a sterling effort to protect those breeds registered by them as pure-bred dogs.

Many dog newspapers and other periodicals used by breeders for advertising their stock in England will no longer accept any advertisement regarding the Pitbull. Consequently, some owners of this breed are advertising the Pitbull as a 'Staffordshire Terrier', and the unwary customer, wishing to purchase a Staffordshire Bull Terrier, may find his money has bought a pup that instead of being an adult 14in to 16in (36cm to 41cm) has grown into a Pitbull of 18in to 20in (46cm to 51cm).

It is wise, therefore, to make sure that when buying a dog through an advertisement, you keep in mind that there is no breed of dog called Staffordshire Terrier. There is a breed American Staffordshire Terrier, a respected breed registered by the American Kennel Club since the 1930s and not used for fighting. There is also the breed American Pitbull Terrier that is registered with the United Kennel Club which provides Championship Shows and has banned any dog known to have been fought from registration and entry to the show ring. Therefore, any buyer of a Pitbull should determine whether it is registered with the United Kennel Club; if it is not, you cannot be sure that you have not bought a dog bred from fighting stock.

In his book on the Bull Terrier, Sir Richard Glynn stated that prior to The Kennel Club's recognition of our breed, many people had ordered Bull Terriers and received Staffordshire Bull Terriers, the latter then carrying the reputation of an aggressive dog. It was in this way that both authors became owners of their first Staffordshire Bull Terriers. Although initially disappointed, we have blessed our good fortune to be owners of this wonderful breed and have never changed to another.

Therefore, if you want a Staffordshire Bull Terrier, go to a reputable and knowledgeable breeder. The vast majority of breeders are great enthusiasts whose interest extends far beyond just showing and breeding. Their main effort is constantly to improve the breed and, if one studies the tremendous strides in popularity that this breed has enjoyed in recent years, there can be no doubt of the success of their policies. The greatest danger now is that with this great popularity there comes demand and a high price for puppies. Fortunately, as yet we have not had the large commercial breeder in our ranks.

Do not hurry your purchase. Look at as many litters as you can. Look at and examine pups and, even if you consider that you have an eye for a dog which may well be true, do not flatter yourself that you can pick the best one after a few minutes' observation. Experts

J. Altoff, one of the best of the breeders in the immediate post-war years.

with many years of breed experience cannot do this with any degree of certainty. If you have previously decided that you prefer a certain colour, you are greatly limiting your field of choice. It is better, in our opinion, to try to select the best-quality puppy you can see, rather than the one whose coat colour appeals to you. We have both owned reds, whites, pieds and brindles of various shades. A hard and fast colour prejudice will limit your choice, and reduce the probability of obtaining a really top-class specimen.

You will naturally find, when viewing a litter, that one will appeal to you more than the others, and, if one you really fancy stands the test of a detailed examination, your instinct may well be right. Alternatively, we think that if there are any whelps in the litter that definitely do not appeal, it would be sensible not to consider them.

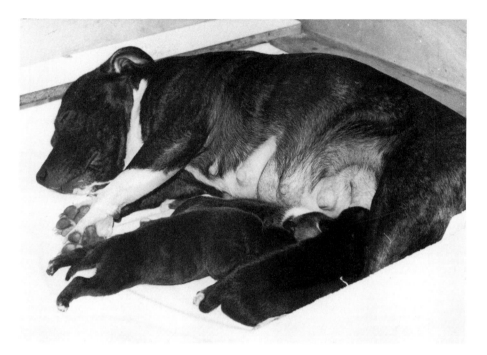

Healthy pups and contented dam. When buying a puppy, always see the dam if possible.

Always ask the breeder if he will let you see the pups exercising out of the whelping box area and, when they are running free and playing fight games, mentally reject any whose movements are not as agile as the others.

Those whose movements you assess as satisfactory should now be examined in more detail. Hold each in turn and examine the physical characteristics of the head. Start with a good look at the eyes, both for colour and placement. You will know that our Standard calls for a dark eye, then greatly extends that restriction by stating that the eye colour may bear some relation to coat colour. What should a white pup's eye colour be? It is our experience and belief that a pup's eye should be as dark as possible and, indeed, we are sure that a light-eyed pup's eyes will not improve with age, rather the reverse. Also the eye shape and placement are important. The eyes should be well rounded, definitely not almond shaped, and should be set wide apart. This, we think, is also of help in

123

At three weeks of age, the pups are beginning to become mobile and to look for trouble.

assessing the strength of head, as eyes that are set well apart are seldom seen in a narrow- or weak-skulled whelp.

If he will stay for long enough, handle the pup's head; it should feel blocky and strong in your hands. Examine the degree of angulation of foreface and skull. In good Stafford pups it often seems that the foreface, or muzzle is at a slightly up-turned angle to the skull, and this is desirable rather than otherwise. The angulation of foreface to skull in an adult should be very much the same, but a slightly upturned angle of the foreface is, in our and probably in most people's opinion, preferable to a slightly downward angle. The head shape of this type is most untypical. Also, the length of foreface in relation to skull should be short, and as wide as it is deep. The foreface always lengthens as the pup grows up, so it is sensible to begin with as short and strong a muzzle as you can get. We have explained in Chapter 2 how difficult it has been, and is, to produce pups with short, strong forefaces, who will retain a level mouth in adulthood.

A dog who has faulty dentition stands little or no chance in the show ring, so obviously it is well worth while to check very carefully the jaw and dentition of your prospective pup. If the underjaw is very strong in proportion to the upper jaw it is quite possible that the adult will become undershot. Examine the teeth carefully and make sure that the upper set of teeth – 'the incisors – are fairly well over the lower ones. By this we do not mean there should be a noticeable gap between the two sets of teeth, but that the upper teeth are obviously over the lower ones. If there is too large a gap, it is an indication that the underjaw, in the adult, will be short and weak – a serious fault. All of the better Stafford breeders have by now, practically eliminated the undershot mouth from their stock, but in a strongly Bull-bred dog like the Stafford it is always possible that this fault will recur in what is in every other way a very promising pup.

The Standard of the breed states that the nose must be black. There is no deviation from this and, ideally, the nose of your prospective purchase must be black. However, in a white or white pied puppy, the nose is often speckled rather than wholly black at this age, and we consider that this should not deter you as, invariably, if the eyes are dark and general health good, in just a few weeks the nose will gradually blacken over, especially if you include a little seaweed powder or other type of iron tonic in his diet. Also, assuming that you are dealing with a breeder, you will have the opportunity of seeing the dam of the litter, and of assuring yourself that she is a good and typical Stafford.

It is well worth while, when looking at the dam, to assess ear carriage and size. It is our opinion that really good ears are small and thin, and fold correctly into the much desired rose ear, i.e. fold back neatly. This ear shape greatly enhances the general appearance of the head. The Standard states that ears should be 'rose or half pricked, and not large'. It goes on to say that full drop or prick ears should be penalized. Generally this clause gives judges considerable latitude and, according to the degree of importance any individual judge considers is correct, he is quite entitled to ignore the size or heaviness of an exhibit's ears as long as they fold correctly.

There is no doubt that, in general, ear size and carriage have improved greatly over the years. Providing the dam has a reasonably correct ear both for size and shape, and realizing that a good breeder would be most unlikely to have used a sire whose ears were faulty, there should be no serious problem with your puppy. During the first few months of a pup's life the ears are likely to lift and drop several times and, until he is nearing adulthood, it is impossible to be certain how they will eventually turn out. On an animal who has a large, well-developed skull, the ears will appear to be smaller than the same ear will look on an animal whose head does not develop so well. It is our opinion as breeders that really good, neat ears are well worth careful consideration in a breeding programme. Once large heavy ears are introduced, they are liable to recur from time to time for some generations.

Examine the legs and feet. The hind legs should, even in a young pup, be true and straight from hip to foot, i.e. parallel to each other. If the hind legs turn in (towards each other) from the hock, regard it as a serious fault. It is an indication that the adult animal will very probably be weak at the back end and will quite probably be cow hocked, a fault that will seriously affect his movement. The bones of all four legs should be well rounded and solid, giving the appearance of being heavy rather than light. At this age the joints tend to be looser than they will be in the adult animal but, making

A three-day-old pup. Note that the nose is not yet coloured black. The pup is red/fawn.

126

allowances for this, a good assessment can be made when the pups are running and playing.

It is difficult, at this age, to assess accurately the spring and depth of rib, as most pups of this age are endowed with a well-sprung and rounded rib-cage, but careful examination will show slight variations in both depth and spring. Hold each pup in turn and carefully feel the body. The pup should feel solid and heavy for his size. Look at the width of each puppy's front, and consider, from both the top and side, both spring and depth. Disregard any amount of fat pups usually carry – you are looking at the ribs, not the meat they may be carrying.

Stand the puppies on a level surface, and look at and compare the length from the base of the neck (withers) to set-on of tail. You will find there are variations, but at this time concentrate only on length and back. If you look at the whole animal, any with a greater depth of rib may well appear shorter because you are looking at the overall animal rather than the back. It is an age-old belief that a short back is usually accompanied by a short tail, and we are sure this is generally true. Do examine the tail, however, and make sure it is free from bone malformations such as kinks or knots, faults that do, for no apparent reason, crop up in our breed. This is a factor inherited from the Bulldog ancestry and is an atavistic trait we do not think will ever be entirely eliminated, especially as breeders now seem to be concentrating on the Bull, rather than the terrier, aspects of the breed.

An adult dog puppy must be an entire animal, both from a breeding and show point of view. This means that in the adult, both testicles will have descended into the scrotum. However, when you are buying a male puppy at about eight weeks of age, it is quite usual that the testicles have not yet dropped. They will normally do so by the third or fourth month, so do occasionally examine your new pup and if, by the time he is, say, four months old, there are no sign of them, or if only one is in evidence, do consult your vet. More often than not a little skilled manipulation will solve the problem.

Sometimes, when you are examining the puppies, some parts of the underparts of the body are a little sore, especially under the forelegs. This is usually due to an over-zealous dam cleaning the pups too enthusiastically, or possibly to being nipped by their litter mates. Normally, when the pup is in his new home, the soreness will disappear within a day or two and is not usually a cause for alarm. More serious would be signs of irritation or soreness which could be caused by fleas or lice. Examine the coat carefully for any signs of fleas or flea dirt. The coat gives a good indication of general health; it should, of course, be short, and in a young pup should be soft and have a shine or bloom.

Often young pups have an umbilical hernia – a small lump on the site of where the cord was – and this is often caused by it being cut too short at the time of birth. Normally, this will reduce as the pup grows, and will have disappeared by the age of about six months. If it should be obstinate, a simple operation is normally all that is required but it would be most unusual if the need for this arose.

Having now examined the pup as well as you can regarding the points we have mentioned, if you decide to buy, you should be getting a strong, healthy youngster who stands a good chance of growing to be an adult who will be a good and typical Stafford. He will well represent the breed and, with kind and considerate training, will give great pleasure to you and your family. He will always try to please, and protect you. Just teach him how.

Dog or Bitch?

Give thought to and decide whether you would prefer a dog or bitch. If you have ambitions to become a breeder eventually, obviously a bitch will be your choice, but it is our opinion that it is probably more difficult to buy a really good-quality bitch puppy than a dog, as many breeders keep the best bitch pup for their own breeding programmes, or place them with acquaintances, with a breeding term arrangement. If you wish to breed and expect to produce good and typical stock, it would be more sensible to try to obtain an animal in excess of about eight months of age. By this age you will be able to assess accurately the quality and soundness of the bitch. In this way, you will probably not be getting a Champion, but will be sure of a good and typical specimen who, if you are thoughtful and sensible in your choice of a sire, will more probably than not produce a litter that is typical and sound, with possibly one or more of the pups, as good or better than your foundation bitch. Remember, though, that most of the litter will be sold to people who want first and foremost a family pet. Make sure that the dog you use, apart from being a typical specimen, is also physically sound. Do not be lured into using a dog who has one outstanding feature, unless he is good 'all over'. Exaggerations of any particular point are not good for any breed, if they are obtained at the expense of balance and soundness.

Whether you decide on a bitch either as a potential breeder, or only as a pet, there are noticeable differences in character between the two sexes. A bitch is invariably softer and more home-loving than a dog. She will be less boisterous and not quite so independent. She will also come into season every six months, during a large part of which time she will have to be watched very carefully, so that she has no chance of meeting a male dog. If by any unfortunate chance the bitch is mated by an unwanted dog, get her to the vet within twenty-four hours. He will give an injection which will terminate the pregnancy. This will also prolong the season but is far better than having an unwanted litter on your hands.

Those of you who decide that they would prefer a dog – and of course, many do – will have an animal that is more of an extrovert, full of fun, and generally more ready to join exuberantly into any family game or situation. He will usually be more independent than a bitch, and, if he can, will be inclined to get out on his own, mainly in order to satisfy an insatiable longing to find and mate a bitch. Even if he becomes a very good specimen who wins at shows and is used as a stud by other breeders, he will always want more and, given any opportunity, will be away on his own.

Pedigree

The United Kingdom

The pedigree of a thoroughbred dog, indeed of any animal with a confirmable history of its ancestry, is purely a document giving the ancestors of the animal to which it refers. Generally, the pedigree of a dog will give from four to six generations and, if it is to be of any value, the sire and dam of the whelp should have their names and title, if applicable, as registered with the Kennel Club entered on the pedigree, plus the registration number and the name and address of the breeder. It will also give the pup's birth date and identifying description of colour or combination of colours.

It is usual that the breeder will register the pup with the Kennel Club, and a certificate of Registration, with the registered number, will be given to the new owner at the time of purchase, along with a transfer form signed by the breeder. This enables the purchaser

The first two known registered Staffordshire Bull Terriers in the USA: Bandits Belle Lettres and Bandits Firestreak Red Rover.

to obtain a registered transfer of ownership by the Kennel Club. At the present time there is a two-tier system of Registration, meaning that the breeder only registers the birth of the whelps, and the new owner, if he wishes to show or breed from his pup when old enough, would be required to extend that type of Registration to 'active' or 'Class 1' Registration. Through the Kennel Club records it is established and guaranteed that the pup is a pure-bred animal of its breed, and that immediate ancestors are also pure bred.

It should be noted that a pedigree is of little use to a novice as it is merely a list of names of dogs, some of whom may well have attained Champion status during their show careers. When a breeder is selling a pup, particularly to a novice, it is often a good sales point to be able to show numbers of Champions in the pedigree, but it is of little use to the novice buyer who will have no knowledge of the named animals' virtues, or even their colour. Both authors firmly believe a 'back-up' pedigree with all informa-tion possible against each dog recorded should be given to the new owner on the purchase of the pup.

130

The vast majority of pups are sold to families who want a pet and who usually buy a pedigree dog after seeing an adult specimen of a particular breed. Generally they simply want a sound healthy pup and have little or no particular interest in showing or breeding the dog. Many owners who do become interested and involved in both showing and breeding often start doing so without any real intention of being anything other than a pet owner, as indeed was the intent of both authors. The breeder invariably will, if the new owner shows interest in becoming an exhibitor in the show ring, give as much information and assistance as possible.

The United States of America

Under the American Kennel Club, the breeder must supply a blue form obtained from them which is the AKC Dog Registration Application Form. This form is the buyer's proof of purchase and transfer of title of the pup to the new owner. It contains information required by the AKC which includes breed, name, registration numbers of sire and dam of that particular litter, date of birth of the litter, and the name and address of the breeder. On the back of the

One of the earliest shows in California before US recognition.

131

form, it must show the name and address of the buyer and the buyer's signature.

The American Kennel Club will then register your pup and send you the Registration Certificate which shows the name of the pup, its breed and colour, and the names of the sire, dam and breeder. It will also record the date of birth and sex, plus the registered number of your pup and the date on which the certificate was issued. You will note that after the registration numbers of sire and dam, there will be two recorded dates, e.g. (10.82) (12.81). This indicates the dates of the issues of the Stud Book Register in which the sire and dam were published by the AKC.

Every transfer of owners must, of course, be recorded, and one should be diligent when filling in the required information. If they wish, the American Kennel Club may cancel registration of a dog and his descendants if the application contains errors or misrepresentation. Fortunately, once having made a stupid error, I found the AKC help more than they cancel!

Breeders are required to keep good records and, to this end, the AKC provides for them a *Dog Ownership and Breeding Records* book. This contains required records of such dogs, records of litters produced and disposition of individual whelps. An authorized representative of the American Kennel Club, such as Area Field Representative, may at any time examine your records, so make sure that they are correct. There are penalties for non-existent or poor record keeping, one being suspension from the privileges of the AKC for failure to observe regulations. When in doubt, the American Kennel Club will give you all the information you need.

4

Care and Management

Puppy Management

Sometimes the actions of dogs are not understood by the owner, particularly an owner new to living with a dog. Let us then discuss a few of the elements of behaviour that will hopefully assist the new owner to understand the actions and, most importantly, the needs of this new pet they have acquired.

The domestic dog (Canis familiaris) is a member of the canine family (Canidae). Canines are classed as mammals (Mammalia), meaning that they possess mammary glands for the nourishment of their young, which are born live. Even after centuries of captivity by man, the dog has retained many of the traits and aspects of social behaviour similar to those of other species classified as Canidae, such as his relative the wolf. A dog that has become feral will revert to the social behaviour patterns of any other animal of the Canidae family. They are essentially pack-hunting animals and therefore if lost, will likely join other homeless dogs in a group under a chosen pack leader. Probably the most basic characteristic of the dog is the desire for companionship from either canine or human, and solitary confinement or isolation is a distressing experience for him. This can be evidenced by a dog continually howling when left alone.

Understandably, then, it can be quite traumatic for a young pup leaving the dam and litter mates and taken to a new and unknown environment. He will miss his litter mates and dam, and can quite easily become upset and frightened by the change. You must, therefore, be gentle with him, forgive and ignore mistakes he makes in the first weeks and try not to leave him for long periods on his own. If it is necessary for you to leave him alone, do confine him in a small area where he will feel safer and do not leave him too often or for lengthy periods of time.

Have his sleeping quarters ready and introduce him to his bed. Encourage and allow him to explore the house and grounds under your supervision. Frequent handling and petting will help a great deal in the transition of the pup from the known to the unknown. If pups are ignored and not handled frequently, especially by the breeder, they may become people-shy so it is not a good idea to leave them alone for long periods of time. The pup can also become hand-shy and, therefore, a lot of gentle petting and handling is required.

An immediate change of diet can upset the digestive ability of the pup. You must ensure that the breeder provides you with a diet sheet and times of feeding. Make sure to keep to that routine until the puppy is well adjusted to his new surroundings. A pup needs four to six small meals a day which can be cut down as he grows until he is an adult. Then he will be on one meal a day or, as some prefer, two meals a day. Do not overfeed your pup: a fat puppy is cute but not healthy.

For a week or so, leave a light on at night-time, or if possible, let your pup sleep in a box in your bedroom where he can hear you and will feel safe. It will be the first time he sleeps alone and not cuddled up to his litter mates. We have found that a good companion for new pups is an alarm clock; the ticking sometimes lulls them to sleep. Make sure his sleeping quarters are draught-free and keep him warm by using a heat-lamp or shredded newspaper that he can burrow under. At this age, it is not wise to give him a blanket that he can get under and so run the risk of suffocation.

Often during this period you will notice bare patches on his coat, primarily on the head and shoulders. This is not uncommon in this breed and is not a serious problem. It is believed to be a teething rash and normally cures itself. However, if the patches persist and become a source of irritation to the pup, you should consult your vet. He will be able to take skin scrapings to analyze and discover if there is a problem. In any event, he will be able to prescribe a soothing medication.

As your pup becomes confident of his surroundings and new family, he will doubtless explore and, if by chance he meets up with your best shoes and damages them, do not punish him, punish yourself! The pup does not know they are your best shoes and the fault is yours for leaving them in an area easily accessible to the pup. A great many of the problems in raising a pup are created by the owner.

Staffordshire Bull Terriers are often referred to as 'Nursemaid' dogs because of their great attachment to children. However, the dog can just as easily be wary of them through the abuse that can be unintentionally administered by a child. Therefore, small children should not be allowed to use the pup as a toy. If the pup is sleeping soundly he should not be disturbed. He needs plenty of sleep when very young. A small child allowed to carry a puppy around can easily drop and injure him, and if the child hurts the pup he might easily give the child an unintentional bite.

Training

Do remember when approaching a pup that his view will be of large feet coming towards him and he can be terrified if you approach with a heavy step. If you want the pup to come to you, squat down on your haunches, put out your hand in a friendly gesture and gently entice him to you, using his name and adding 'Come'. He will soon understand and, without fear, come to you easily. When he does, pet and praise him.

One of the most important words that a new pup must learn is 'No'. You will find yourself using it time after time. The word should be given with strong emphasis and possibly a gentle tap on his nose. Do not come up behind him; always face him, for otherwise you run the risk of having a nervous dog.

The pup must be house-trained. During the day, monitor him and, at regular intervals and definitely after meals, take him to the area you wish him to use and stay with him until he has relieved himself, especially if it is dark, and praise him with 'Good dog'. He will soon learn that using that particular spot pleases you and will continue to use that area. Pups usually give some warning by anxiously looking for a spot and sometimes whimpering. It is wise to put newspaper down next to his sleeping box since in his early stages he will get out of the box and urinate and defecate immediately. Your pup cannot be continent, especially before the age of twelve weeks, and you must watch him constantly.

Once your pup appears to recognize his name when called and is thoroughly adapted to living with you, play games with him that will be fun for him and at the same time teach him basic obedience. This can be done at any time of the day. Walk into another room and call 'Fido, come', with great emphasis on the word 'Come'. Use his name so that he will understand you are referring to him. Continue to call until he finds you, whereupon give him lots of praise and then go off into another room and start the game again.

This well-trained puppy feels confident and secure.

The pup must be lead trained but do not start this too early in his life. We have found it is easier between five and six months, by which time he will have settled down, will be confident and secure and will have learned basic commands, such as 'No' and 'Come'. First, buy a small soft collar. A hard leather collar will probably chafe his neck. Normally, the pup will not like wearing it but leave it on until he has become used to it. When he has taken wearing a

136

collar for granted, latch the lead on to it but do not immediately try to take him for a walk. Let him move around with the lead trailing behind and when he appears to have come to terms with it, you can start to teach him to walk on a collar and lead.

If you have an adult dog, or can persuade a neighbour who has one to help you, more often than not the pup will happily follow the adult and become lead-trained naturally and quickly. I had great difficulty persuading my bitch to walk on a lead until Steve Stone, her breeder, brought the pup's sire and dam to walk with her. Immediately she was quite happy to trot between them and I had no further problem. Do not drag the pup along and do not discipline him. Encouragement is the name of the game in lead training and it should start with very short exercises.

Once he has become acquainted with the lead and decides he likes going out for a walk, he will probably then be very enthusiastic and want to pull you along, which is as bad as refusing to walk. Be patient and keep encouraging him but do not drag him back to you. Stop and gently pull him toward you using the word 'Come' and do not move until he is beside you; then start the lesson over again.

Over the years, we have found that dogs are scavengers, particularly when young. So, watch your pup carefully, particularly when you are walking him or when he is in your garden alone. Do not keep any harmful objects that he can find in an open cupboard or rubbish container. Make sure he receives all necessary medical care and constantly have him examined to keep him free from parasites. If you have to leave him alone, make sure he is confined in an area where he cannot harm himself. Never leave him alone in the house for extended periods of time. If possible, take him with you and, most important, do not use physical punishment. You will get better results by shaming him by the tone of your voice. Take care of your pup and protect him. We know that in return, as an adult dog, he will protect and take care of your family.

The Adolescent and Adult Dog

Your dog is now in adolescence. He is neither a puppy nor an adult dog and this is the time for you to forgive a lot and teach a lot. It is to be hoped he will have given up chewing your shoes, eating everything that is not good for him and knows his family and his name. During this period of time in his life he will act like an adult dog but frequently revert to acting like a puppy. He will also have an enormous amount of energy!

If you have given him a great deal of attention throughout puppyhood, he will be attached to you, will feel secure, aim to please you and rely upon you. At this age he will be venturesome, impetuous and exhibiting *joie de vivre*, and will probably do stupid things that will make you laugh and occasionally make you angry.

Now is the time to start moulding him into the adult dog you want him to be, and this must be done through obedience training. If you are seriously interested in competing in obedience trials, we suggest that it is far better to join an Obedience Club. There are specific requirements and routines for Obedience Classes in the show ring and trials.

For the dog that is your pet and companion it is best to train him yourself to the type of obedience you will require from him. The secret is that you *want* your dog to *want* to please you by doing exactly what you *want* him to do. Therefore, do not use the praise and punishment theory of training. Obedience means you have a dog you can live with, rely upon in any situation and, for the dog, confidence and security. If he is always receiving punishment for wrongdoing, he will have little confidence, will be nervous and probably shy, and if you constantly bribe him he will only obey when bribed. There is nothing wrong with a goodie as a reward but it should not be connected with training. We have found that verbal praise should be given when he has done something you want him to do and verbal discipline when he does not obey.

The three most important commands are 'Sit', 'Stay' and 'Come'. he may have learned 'Come' during puppyhood but now it must be reinforced. Do not be too serious about training. If your dog is taking a little longer to understand than you feel he should, do not get frustrated. Repetition and patience is the name of the game.

The command 'Sit' is a very easy one for the dog to understand and you should start with that. When he is standing still, gently press the rear quarters to the sit position and use the word 'Sit' as you do this. When you are feeding him, tell him 'Sit' before you put his food bowl down. If you are going to give him a treat, hold it in front of his nose and demand 'Sit'. You will be very surprised how quickly he will understand that command. Always use his name before you give the command.

The command 'Stay' will not be so easy for your dog. You should start by putting your hand in front of you with the palm facing the dog and, with emphasis, use the word 'Stay'. Do not, at this time, move yourself. If the dog moves, take him back to the spot where you originally put him on 'Stay' and start the exercise over again. At first, do not expect too much from him. When you are confident that he will stay providing you are standing watching him, you can start walking backwards, still facing him, with the palm of your hand in front of you facing him, and continue to remind him that he is on 'Stay'. Each step you take while he remains on the 'Stay' command is a step he is taking to understand what is required by you.

When your dog appears to be thoroughly familiar with this part of the exercise, you should start walking away from him with your back towards him. More often than not, you will find he immediately breaks. I had this particular problem with Piltdown Bill, our model for this book, who came to me as an adult, and his 8-month-old son who was only just beginning to learn obedience. They would happily and with great confidence stay on command if I was standing in front of them. However, as soon as I turned my back and walked away, they both immediately broke and came rushing after me. I realized this was probably caused by their fear of being abandoned.

Sometimes when you get to the point of resistance by a dog, young or old, a bit of imagination from the trainer can help. After many fruitless efforts, I decided to carry a small mirror with me, put both dogs on 'Stay' and walk away, monitoring their actions by watching them in the mirror. At the first movement from either of them and without turning around to face them, I commanded, 'Stay'. I must admit I spoiled the first effort by laughing at the expression on their faces and they, of course, broke the 'Stay'. Both were totally confused and forevermore were quite convinced that I had eyes in the back of my head. After that, it was quite easy to keep them on 'Stay' whether or not I was facing them, had my back to them or was totally out of sight of them. They were now confident that I was not deserting them.

It is a good idea when training your dog to use hand and arm signals as well as verbal commands. There may be a time when your dog is too far away from you to hear the commands and may possibly be in trouble. Once when climbing down one of the Hollywood Hills with my four dogs, I left Tinkinswood Imperial at the top where I presume he was visiting his coyote friends, and I

Make training a game for the dog to enjoy.

and my other dogs started down without him expecting him to catch up with us. The area is host to rattlesnakes and, using toy snakes, I had taught all my dogs the danger of attacking or getting too close to a snake. Half-way down the hill I discovered a very large rattlesnake curled up on our path and, naturally, we backed up and came down by another route. I knew Fred could smell out a rattlesnake with little effort and he often warned me with a peculiar warning bark. However, I was worried that he would come barrelling down the path to catch up with us and run into the snake. I also knew I could not climb back up to that spot quickly enough to stop him, so when he appeared I decided to use hand signals from a distance and successfully led him to another path and brought him down safely. A man walking by stopped to watch this procedure and was so impressed that he decided he ought to get himself 'one of them ugly-looking dogs'!

As your adolescent dog reaches the status of adult you will find he will become more mature and will be thinking for himself. Therefore, training him to advanced stages will become easier. He will be able to discern between friend and foe and will be a good guard dog for you, your family and home. He will also become more sedate in his attitudes and actions. We have discovered that dogs have a need to be part of your family, so why not take him out in the car whenever it is possible, take him walking every day and treat him to special and favourite foods now and again?

Nutrition

We are well aware that good nutrition is most important to the health of the dog. Dogs are by the structure of their teeth carnivorous animals but zoologists also regard them as omnivorous, i.e. like humans they will eat vegetation as well as meat and accept a variety of food. They are, indeed, wonderful scavengers!

We are all aware that treats should be nourishing but a happy dog is the one who occasionally shares 'goodies' with its owner – but we do mean *occasionally*. Personally, we have always found that the quickest way to train a dog and win everlasting affection and loyalty is by the occasional treat and not the choke-chain. We find nothing wrong with occasional treat sharing. What we do find wrong is overfeeding through too much sharing and lack of knowledge of content and size of the main diet, plus lack of exercise. It appears to us that many owners keep to one type of food with little variation which, even though nutritious, must become monotonous and uninteresting to the dog. After all, if our diet consisted of one daily meal of a juicy steak, we would soon hate the butcher!

Vitamins and minerals are essential to the maintenance of a dog's health and need not be a mystery to owners. There are excellent publications that deal with their functions and food sources to guide owners wishing to prepare their own dog food, as many do. Fortunately for dog and owner, there are excellent prepared foods containing all the ingredients that make for a healthy pet, providing you do not overdo the amount given. The primary problem for most owners is knowing how much food their dog needs to maintain good health. The energy level the dog has is derived from the food he eats, which mainly depends on the activity level of the animal.

The amount you feed your dog should be adjusted to maintain optimum body weight. The optimum weight is when the ribs cannot be easily seen but can be easily felt. General activity level, temperament and environment must be taken into consideration. Poor feeding will show in a poor coat, and the quality and amount of food can result in bloat. If the dog is fed in a single large meal per day, particularly through poorly digestible diets, the tissues supporting the stomach will allow twisting to occur. It is believed that excessive calcium may lead to changes in the stomach and be linked to bloat. Different pets have different nutritional needs and the diet you feed is important to their good health.

Energy provided by food is measured by the number of heat units (calories) that arise from burning off protein, carbohydrates and fats. A simple way of determining the calorie count of a meal – especially if using canned dog food that indicates percentage of protein, carbohydrate and fat – is to multiply the percentage of protein and carbohydrate by four and the percentage of fat by nine. When burned, a gram of protein and a gram of carbohydrate produces four calories and fat, nine calories. There are 454 grams to the pound, so add the calories and multiply the total by 4.5; the answer will show the calorific count of the meal. Meat, depending upon the cut, is approximately 20 per cent protein and half that amount of fat and contains no carbohydrates. How many calories per pound weight are required by the average Staffordshire Bull Terrier? A 30lb (14kg) dog requires 1250 calories per day. A 40lb dog (18kg) dog requires 1500 calories per day. From this you should be able to ascertain the requirements of your own dog.

Obesity is the most common nutritional disease. An excess of

Norman Berry's dogs are always shown in good condition. The result of correct feeding and exercise.

143

fatty tissue may be associated with health problems. It is believed that overweight pets generally have more physical ailments and thus a shorter life than those of average and correct weight. Obesity predisposes your pet to many problems, i.e. breathing difficulty, heart disease, liver disease, heat intolerance, to name a few, and, of course, the animal is usually irritable because of discomfort.

The cause is often simply overeating and under-exercising. Dogs must have exercise, and good free-running in rough terrain is wonderful for their health. It is possible to exercise a dog simply by throwing a ball. The official yardage of a mile in both the UK and USA is 1,760 yards (1.6km). Measure the yards you can throw a ball. The dog will gallop to the ball and trot back with it to you, doubling the yardage you have thrown. Divide this yardage into the length of the mile and you will know how many times you must throw the ball to give the dog one mile of exercise.

However, if this type of exercise is all your dog will ever get, particularly if always in your own backyard, you are not being a very good owner. A dog, particularly a male, must have stimulus, and boredom can easily produce disease. Many males suffer from satyriasis (exaggerated sexual desire) caused by boredom and lack of stimulating exercise, and if you own more than one dog, you will, no matter what the breed, have problems between them. Correct nutrition, and good exercise routines go together to keep your dog healthy and happy.

5

Showing and Judging

As your dog approaches maturity, it is quite possible you will consider that he is developing into a really good specimen, and will wish to get general recognition of his quality. Obviously the only way in which you may get public recognition is by entering him at dog shows, where he can compete and be compared with other animals of similar age to himself.

Before you may enter a show, however, you have to apply to the Kennel Club to have the dog entered on to the Class One Active Register, which will entitle you to enter any type of show sanctioned by the KC. (At birth, the breeder will have registered the puppy with the Kennel Club, but this will be a Class Two Registration).

Also, it is very probable, and certainly very sensible, that before deciding your dog is of show quality, you will have attended some shows at which Staffords have been exhibited and mentally compared the animals entered in the appropriate classes with your own dog. Without doubt, at this time you will meet spectators with whom you can discuss the virtues and faults of the animals being exhibited; indeed, you will find it impossible to stop some of them, and you will quickly begin to realize that there are considerable differences of opinion as to which should and should not be the winner.

You will also hear some criticisms of the judge, and these do at times seem to have some justification. Do realize from the start that this happens, to a greater or lesser degree, at all shows and is bound so to do. The Standard of any breed can be, and is, interpreted in different ways, and any individual is likely to give more emphasis to those clauses which he considers to be the most important. Always remember, no written words can illustrate a complete picture of the live animal, and the only parts of the Standard which should be completely observed – but are often ignored – are the restrictive clauses such as the height and weight (*see* Chapter 2).

Each judge is quite entitled and, indeed, is honour bound, to give

Ch. Bunninjong Caesar. This red dog was a natural for shows, and was handled expertly by the late Harry Foulks.

his own opinion regarding the physical and mental attributes of the animals before him, and to put up what is, in his opinion, the nearest to the ideal. We consider it important to keep this in mind, for if you decide to show your dog, and the judge decides to pass him by, another judge, on another day, may decide quite differently. Also, dog showing is bound to contain elements of luck and, if at any time the judge happens to be looking at any particular animal when he is standing perfectly and right on top of his form, it will immediately create a favourable impression. Of course, the exact reverse may be the case, and it stands to reason that a well-trained dog, who is well handled, must stand a better chance than one whose owner has not bothered to train his dog to show. Always try to watch both the dog and the judge – this is difficult, we know, especially in a big class, but well worthwhile. You have entered your dog to win, and should show that you are confident he is the best one there. Never stop trying.

The Stafford is one of the easiest of all the breeds to prepare for the show ring, so be sure he is as well presented as possible. Assuming that he is well exercised and in good health, his coat will be naturally glossy and, if you give him a rub over every day with a hound glove or stiff brush, you will enhance this and also keep his skin clean. A polish with a chamois leather or a piece of velvet before entering the ring will give a little extra sheen.

Train your dog to stand correctly on a loose lead, so that the judge may see and assess him easily. There seems to be a tendency among many exhibitors to kneel down and 'prop' their dog. This should not be done and, indeed, is not necessary if your animal is well constructed and has good conformation. Your dog will look much better standing free. Many judges look unfavourably upon over-handling and, in our opinion, it is a tendency which should be discouraged. We assume that you give your dog enough exercise to keep his toe-nails short, so that the only other thing you may need to do is tidy up his tail. Many Staffords tend to grow rather long hair, usually on the underside of the tail. This should be trimmed off, preferably with a pair of blunt-ended scissors. Take care not to over-trim though, because a 'rat' tail is as unsightly as a bushy one. Either tends to spoil the picture of balance you require.

You can complement your dog by the clothing you wear so leave the jeans and sweatshirts at home. Inappropriate attire can ruin the picture of the dog and handler and certainly does not compliment the Judge. If handling a dark-coated dog, it is better to give contrast by light-coloured clothing or by dark clothing if the dog has a light-coloured coat. Be sure to wear shoes that are comfortable and appropriate. If the Show is held outdoors on wet grass or inside on a slippery floor, you will need shoes that provide good traction. For this breed, ladies would be well advised to wear flat or low-heeled shoes.

When competing at a show, always allow yourself plenty of time. If it is not a benched show, which is quite usual at both Limit and Open Shows, find the quietest place available to make any final preparations, and ensure that both you and your dog are calm and confident. This is the time when a crate is invaluable. The judge might be behind on his schedule, causing a delay in the time your breed will be judged and it is better for the dog to be crated where he can rest or have a snooze and be kept out of the way of other exhibits. Do not forget to take him for a walk before entering the ring to allow him, if necessary, to relieve himself. We can assure you that there is nothing more embarrassing to a handler than an

147

exhibit stopping in the ring to do what comes naturally, and we doubt the judge will be too impressed by this behaviour. Go with the intention of winning. Second place, or worse, is not what you came for. Try all the time and, even if your cause seems to be lost on this particular day, it is, or should be, good training for both of you which may well pay off at future shows.

United Kingdom Shows
(V.H. Pounds)

When you enter the ring, the steward will place you in the correct position, and usually the judge will walk along the line-up, making his first assessment. He will then go to the most convenient place – invariably the left centre – of the ring, and examine each animal individually. Most judges give a thorough examination, and your dog must be trained to stand still and correctly while being handled. After this examination you will be required to 'move' your dog in order to show soundness of construction and that he moves correctly in the way instructed by the Standard. Often the judge will wish to look at the dog's movement from the side as well as away and towards him, and will probably require you to move him twice. We have explained in Chapter 2 (*see* pages 102–6) how much the head carriage affects this. Make sure he holds his head fairly high and strides out proudly and purposefully.

After being examined, return to your original place and rest your dog if possible, though remembering to keep an eye on the judge. When all the dogs in the class have been examined and returned to their places, the judge will walk slowly along the line-up, making his final assessment. This is a time for your dog to be looking at his best, and good training is often fully rewarded. After standing about for a long time, suffering the indignity of being handled by a complete stranger, and generally being bored stiff, many dogs become restive and show badly, which must lessen their chances. We are sure the general standard of handling has not improved during the last few years, and a really well-trained dog who shows *all* the time has a much greater chance than rivals who may, in themselves, be just as good-quality dogs, but do not show so well.

At some of the Open and at all the Championship Shows, benches are provided, and at this type of show, your show pass will include a bench number, which you will find corresponds to a number on

This dog, Trebboe Jake the Rake, was always handled and shown well by Len Masterman. He won mainly under all-round judges.

one of the benches at the show. All breeds have a section of benches allotted to them so, on arrival, enquire from one of the show marshals – or another Stafford exhibitor, if you see one – where the Stafford benches are, and you will find your bench in that section. It is mandatory to have a benching chain, and you will find a ring at the back of the bench, onto which you will clip one end of your chain with, of course, your dog at the other. Ensure that the chain is not so long that it allows your dog to get his head round to the next bench, or so short that he cannot lie down and relax in comfort. Bring a rug or blanket, and make sure he is as comfortable as possible. Be sure to bring food and a water bowl for him, because most benched shows are all-day affairs. You will also probably use the bench for storage of your personal possessions – very sensible, providing you leave enough room for the dog!

If you are going to be away from your bench for any length of time, make sure you have a friend, or an exhibitor on an adjoining bench, who will watch your dog for you. You are entirely responsible for his safety and well-being. During the last few years, several Staffords have been stolen, despite being benched. Our breed is the most popular and one of the most valuable of all the terrier breeds at the moment, and may well be a target for persons 'on the make'.

There are, at the time of writing, seventeen specialist Staffordshire Bull Terrier clubs in Great Britain, and in whichever part of the country you live, there is quite near you a club which caters for both the dog and owner. All of them hold training classes and 'teach-ins', and hold at least three shows a year, usually one of each class, i.e. one Limit Show, at which only club members are eligible to enter, one Open and one Championship Show, both of which are open to all. You will find the members friendly and very helpful, and we strongly advise you to join your local club. You will find friends and the companionship of fellow enthusiasts who are genuinely interested in the well-being of this wonderful breed. A list of UK Clubs and the addresses of their secretaries can be found in Useful Addresses (*see* page 235).

United States of America Shows
(Lilian Rant)

Before you enter a Championship Show competition, you will need to concentrate on training your dog to the required routine of showing and it would be wise to enter into several matches for practice for yourself and your exhibit. Matches are very informal and designed to be a learning experience for both dog and exhibitor. The entry fees are usually very reasonable and you will be judged mostly by handlers and knowledgeable and experienced breeders and exhibitors. There are also many AKC Championship judges who give their time to judging matches, particularly for new breeds. If you make mistakes in a match you need not feel at all uncomfortable or embarrassed by either your performance or that of your exhibit. From these judges you will invariably be given all the help and advice that you need. These matches are called 'fun matches' and, for the most part, they really are very enjoyable.

When you feel confident of yourself and your exhibit and believe your dog is of sufficient quality and training to compete in a Championship Show, a premium list and entry form will be sent to you on request at least five weeks prior to the closing date of the

Expert handling is essential in the USA and many professional handlers are employed. This photograph is of Bob Jordan showing Ch. Silverlake Gypsy Queen. Before retirement, Mr Jordan was one of the top handlers in the USA.

entries. The premium list will contain such information as the names of the officers of the All Breed Kennel Club sponsoring the event, the veterinarian who will be present at the Show, the names and addresses of the judges and the breeds they will be judging, and whether or not the Show is benched. You will complete the requirements of the entry form and in turn will receive notification

151

of the number of the ring for your breed, the time of judging and usually directions to the show site.

The Ring Steward will give you an arm band showing the number that has been allotted to your exhibit and this is worn on your left arm. Be ready to enter the ring promptly when the class is called. Remember that the judge has probably more breeds to judge and is on a time schedule.

When entering the ring, look confident and proud, even though your exhibit may not have earned one single ribbon at a previous show. This might just be your day! If it is the first time you are entering the Big Ring, try not to be nervous. Your feelings can easily be transmitted to your exhibit who might then not show himself as well as he could.

Quite often the judge will first require all dogs in the class to gait in a circle around the ring. He will be assessing each dog for

In the USA the appearance of the handler, as well as the dog, is important.

movement, drive, topline, balance and head carriage. Move your dog at his best pace, keeping your place in the line and be sure your dog is inside the circle, between you and the judge. Be courteous and do not run into the exhibitor in front of you. If you are being crowded, either step outside the circle to make it larger or move slightly inside the circle.

The first rule of showing that you should remember is that the dog must be presented to the judge and not the judge to the dog. This means that your exhibit must be thoroughly trained to the required routine of physical body examination. If your dog will not stand still, the judge cannot judge him, so remember that presentation is extremely important.

The only time your dog is required to work is in the show ring and it is of short duration and not exactly arduous for him. Therefore, stack and pose your dog properly and do not allow him to relax. During the examination try to keep yourself out of the judge's way. If he is examining the head, stand at the rear of your dog and as he continues to move around the dog, keep moving to the opposite side. Do not speak to the judge unless spoken to; allow him to concentrate on his job.

After he has examined the dog, he will require you to move the dog to assess his movement. Listen carefully to his instructions and follow them. Judges vary in the manner they wish to have the dog moved. He may want the exhibit to move down and back in a straight line and, if so, be sure you line your dog up with the judge. He may want you to move in a triangle, meaning moving your dog up the ring to the first corner, across the end of the ring to the opposite corner and back to the judge by a diagonal line. He may want you to gait your dog on a straight line away from him at the side of the ring to the corner, across to the opposite corner, back to the first corner and straight back to the judge (though this is rare). Remember, when moving your exhibit for the judge to assess the movement, you have his undivided attention, so make the most of it. Move your dog with purpose and with confidence.

After examining your exhibit, the judge will move on to the next dog. This is not a reason for you to relax your dog unless the judge has indicated that you may. Even then it is not a good idea. There might well be a time when the judge is examining a dog and looking back to compare it with another dog that interests him and that he has already examined. The latter might well be your exhibit, so keep him working.

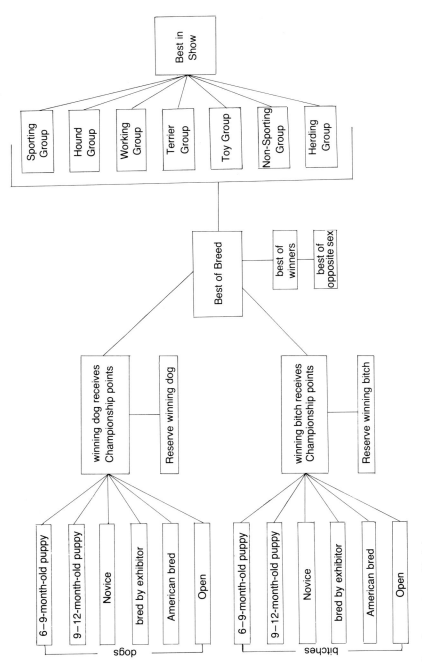

American system of judging.

154

At no time should you try to fool or outwit the judge. Remember, judges were exhibitors long before they became judges and know all the tricks of the trade! When all breeds entered into the show have been judged and the Best of Breed Awards have been made, Group Classes are held. There is no obligation for you to stay for Group Classes and Best in Show. However, be a good sport and, as an owner of your particular breed, stay for the Group judging to give support to your Breed's Winning Dog.

Do not forget to congratulate your dog. Take him home and give him his favourite dinner. He did his best for you!

Classes

The seven regular classes offered to exhibitors by the American Kennel Club are Puppy, Twelve to Eighteen Months, Novice, Bred-by-Exhibitor, American-bred, Open and Winners. All classes are divided by sex.

Puppy Class   This Class is for dogs of six months of age and over but they must be under twelve months of age and may not be Champions. The puppy's age is calculated up to and including the first day of the show in which he is entered. A dog whelped on 1 January is eligible to compete in a Puppy Class at a show on the first day of July and may continue to compete in that class up to and including 31 December of that year. Beyond that day, the pup will not be eligible to be entered into this Class.

Twelve to Eighteen Months   This class is provided at Specialty Shows that must be held apart from an all-breed event. Age calculation is the same as for the Puppy Class, i.e. a dog whelped on 1 January may compete in this class on 1 January of the following year and continue up to and including 30 June of that year.

Novice Class   Dogs entered in this Class must be six months of age and over and have been whelped in the United States of American or Canada. Prior to the closing date of entries, the dog must not have won three first prizes in the Novice Class, a first prize in the Bred-by-Exhibitor Class, American Bred or Open Classes, nor earned points toward Champion status.

Bred by Exhibitor Class The dog must be six months of age or over and may not be a Champion. He must have been whelped in either the United States of America, or whelped in Canada if individually registered in The American Kennel Club Stud Book. The dog must be six months of age or over, may not be a Champion and must be owned wholly or in part by the person or spouse of the person who was the breeder or one of the breeders of record. The dog must be handled in the show ring by the breeder or one of the breeders of record or by a member of the immediate family of the breeder or of one of the breeders of record. This is an excellent class for breeders to show the quality of stock they are producing.

American-Bred Class This class is open for dogs of six months of age and over; they may not be Champions and must have been whelped in the United States of America by reason of a mating that took place in the United States of America. This is an important class to introduce and establish a 'new' breed as an American-bred specimen, and in the earlier days of our breed we failed to use it to our advantage.

Open Class This is open for any dog of six months of age and over, except in a member Specialty Club Show held *only* for American-bred dogs, and therefore, the Open Class shall be only for American-bred dogs.

Winners Class This class is allowed only at shows where American-Bred and Open Classes are held. There is no entry fee for Winners Class competition. The dog or bitch must earn the right to compete in this Class. The Class is divided by sex and opened only to undefeated dogs of the same sex who have won first prizes in either Puppy, Twelve-to-Eighteen Months, Novice, Bred-by-Exhibitor, American-Bred and Open Classes.

After the judge has selected his Winners Dog and Winners Bitch, those dogs leave the ring, and the dog and bitch awarded second place in their classes compete for Reserve Winners Dog and Reserve Winners Bitch. The Winners Dog and Winners Bitch then compete against the Champions of Record for Best of Breed. If the Winners Dog or Winners Bitch is awarded Best of Breed, he or she is automatically awarded Best of Winners, otherwise, the Winners Dog and Winners Bitch are judged together for Best of Winners following the judging for Best of Breed.

For Champion status a dog or bitch must earn 15 points and cannot earn more than 5 points at any show. The number of points that can be earned at any one show depends upon the number of exhibits in each sex. For Champion status, a dog or bitch must earn two Majors, meaning 3 or 5 points; these numbers are decided by the American Kennel Club, based on average entries for a breed throughout the year. The remaining number of required points may be earned singly. However, each sex can often take points from the other. As an example, if the Winners Bitch has earned 5 points at a show and the Winners Dog 3 points, if the Winners Dog beats the Winners Bitch for Best of Winners, the dog will take the difference between the bitch's points and his points earned, meaning both will then have 5 points (a Major). By this system, the number of points awarded toward Champion status depends entirely upon the number of dogs in competition.

Judging
(V.H. Pounds)

Why and how does any person become a judge? Why is it that judges are willing and eager to work very hard in order to inflict their opinion of the dogs on the exhibitors who, in turn, are very willing and able to assess critically and otherwise (and invariably vocally) the opinions of the judge? Without doubt, there are many laudable reasons. I can only write of my own feelings in this area and hope that the opinions I give may be of some use and may help maintain and, hopefully, even improve the general quality of the Staffordshire Bull Terrier as a very desirable show dog and pet.

I had owned and shown Staffordshire Bull Terriers for nearly twenty years before becoming a judge of the breed and, quite honestly, had no ambition or real desire to do so. An old friend pushed me into judging the breed at an Open Show of the all-breed club of which she was a committee member. The club contemplated dropping Staffordshire Bull Terriers from their schedule. My friend, rightly or wrongly, insisted that I would draw a good paying entry which would persuade the club to retain the breed at their shows.

Having agreed to accept the assignment, doubts and misgivings started to plague me. Would I miss a good specimen, or cross over, or commit some other unforgivable sin that would quickly end my career as a show judge? I do not know if all new judges are worried before their first show. I do know life was for me very miserable during the week or so before the engagement, and the closer the date, the more apprehensive I became.

The great day arrived and, after all due preliminaries, I was facing my first judging assignment. Within a few minutes, all my doubts and fears were forgotten. I became so absorbed in correctly assessing and comparing the differing degrees of virtue of the exhibits before me, that I was completely in a world of my own, out of touch with everything except the task I had accepted. I thoroughly enjoyed the experience and when it was over thought what an idiot I had been in avoiding any suggestion given to me to become a judge. I decided I should have started judging years ago!

After the judging, when mentally assessing my performance, although I was satisfied with my decisions and very appreciative of the kind encouragement given by some of the exhibitors (albeit mainly the winners), I realized that many losers were anything but happy. Reflecting upon this, I found it did not bother me at all. I was confident about my placings and on that day I was the judge and, therefore, my opinion of the exhibits before me was the one that mattered.

Although I was pleased with my decisions, I was not nearly so enthused with my method, or rather lack of method, of judging. I had not realized how essential it is to instil in oneself a consistent and correct method of examination of a dog. I remembered examining an exhibit's head and body but after going over several other dogs, I realized I had neglected to examine the dentition on the first dog. This was bad judging and I knew that if I wished to be successful as a judge I would have to consider much more carefully a sequence of examination that would give me the confidence that I had been thorough, had not missed anything and would, therefore, make accurate assessment of the virtues of one dog in comparison with all the others in the class.

I doubt there is a judge anywhere who, on reflection, does not have some second thoughts on the decisions made, but I learned the only person I had to satisfy and please was myself. Judging any form of livestock for cosmetic quality is always one individual's opinion, whatever breed of animal is being judged, and that opinion is invariably influenced by many factors. Often it may be a 'type' closest in physique to the one that the judge has at home, or based on early experiences in the breed, the time when a prospective good breeder and potential judge is, as a novice, very receptive to the opinions voiced by more experienced and established breed specialists. This must be a good foundation in many ways, but always with the proviso that the ideal specimen of one's imagination must also be an animal who physically and mentally illustrates most closely the dictates of the Standard of the breed.

It behoves a potential judge who wishes to be efficient to regard and study three main requirements. Firstly, there must be total knowledge of the directive of the Breed Standard and how best to apply that Standard to the living specimen. I found the most satisfactory way to do this was to watch very carefully the exhibits I saw in the ring and on the benches and to consider, in my own mind, which was the nearest to the ideal I would like to breed, always bearing in mind they also had to conform to the limitations of the Standard.

When I started in this breed, the original Standard was still being used and, consequently, 17in (43cm) dogs were often winning top awards. I realized, however, in common with most other Stafford fanciers, that the new (1948) Standard would, in the near future, have to be observed and the dog and bitch I admired most must conform in every way to the new requirements. I think any breeder must have an ideal to aim at, and Ch. Sandras Boy and Ch. Brinstock Sandy Bridget were the Staffords nearest to my ideal. I know I thought that if I could breed animals to their standard, I would be more than satisfied. I have never forgotten either of them and a clear mental picture of both remains with me. Probably they have influenced my judging and, if so, it must have been for the good.

Secondly, thorough assimilation of knowledge of bone and muscle structure must be attained and the correct placement and operation expected of them. By this I do not intend to imply that I have always had an in-depth knowledge of the anatomy of the dog nor learned, parrot-fashion, the names of the bones and muscles in order to impress the novice. As an example, I knew there was a very strong muscle from the poll via the neck to the shoulders and that it gave shape and support for the head carriage. Until researching for this book I did not know it was called the *ligamentum nuchae* or that it was a ligament rather than a muscle. The significant thing was that I knew it was there and the way it operated. Any competent judge should learn how the skeleton is put together and how it is activated and held by muscles.

Thirdly, one must examine each dog to ensure that faults, virtues and unsoundness are revealed and obviously it means working

Ch. Black Tusker. Probably the most admired Staffordshire Bull Terrier in the breed's history. He fitted the Standard very closely and is the most dominant stud dog the breed has yet produced.

from front to back. Personally, I first have a very good look at the animal from the front, rear and both sides. I include both sides since our breeds' coloration often carries markings and I have found a surprising difference in the impression of shape that can occur in, say, a dog whose head is brindle and white on one side and solid brindle on the other.

One must methodically check the entire dog, which obviously means working from front to back. Examine the head from both front and side, noting the size of nostrils and strength of foreface – particularly the underjaw strength – and decide if the dog is 'lippy'. Examine the placement, size and coloration of the eyes, the shape of skull relative to foreface and the size, fold and thickness of the

160

ears. Do not forget carriage of head and general expression since a Staffordshire Bull Terrier should be completely confident and self-contained, and expression and manner will give a good indication of correct temperament. Examine dentition thoroughly. As we have stated, all too often the examination of the mouth is very limited and inadequate, and our study of the Standard explains why it is important (*see* pages 59–64).

Study the construction of this breed so that you will automatically recognize when the neck moulds properly into the shoulder, the length and strength of muscles holding the shoulder in, the straightness and quality of bone, width of front, correct rib-cage and sound hindquarters. I have found that looking down on the dog will enable you to assess spring of rib, set of shoulder and elbows, strength of loin, placement and size of pelvis, From the rear, view the strength and straightness of the legs plus placement in relation to the front legs. The balance of the dog is of utmost importance. The movement of the dog is dealt with in Chapter 2 (*see* pages 100–9) and, although some directive is given in the present Standard, most judges accept the importance of this factor and also

Ch. Fulfin Black Eagle. Similar to his sire, Ch. Black Tusker, in make and shape.

161

realize that Stafford movement is, because of the specialized construction, quite different from that of the other breeds in the Terrier Group.

A judge must learn to keep a picture in mind of the virtues of each dog examined. Here I say virtues since it is my opinion that all exhibits should primarily be judged on virtues and then these should be weighed against the severity of the faults. Generally, the breed today is much more uniform and sounder than when I started seriously studying the dog forty years ago. Progress depends upon continuous concentration on general improvement and judges have a serious responsibility in making sure that the progress is maintained.

It should be remembered that in the United Kingdom, since the breed's recognition by the Kennel Club, we have been fortunate to have had a great number of specialist breed judges whose whole-hearted devotion has been to the breed, contributing greatly to its progress. This is in no way meant to imply that the all-rounder judges have not also made a great contribution to the breed. Indeed, the all-rounder, whose emphasis is usually on physical balance, soundness of construction and movement, provided a beneficial counter-balance to the specialist judge whose opinion of merit is sometimes based on greater appreciation of more specialized physical virtues. In the United States, where the breed is judged almost 100 per cent by all-round judges, progress has not, in my opinion, been as marked and breed type is not nearly as uniform. Bad judging and breeding through lack of in-depth knowledge spells disaster in uniformity of a breed.

6

Breeding

All pure-bred dogs have a pedigree, the proof of lineage, and should be registered with a Kennel Club. The purpose of the pedigree is to record the ancestry of both the sire and dam of the offsprings. On reading the pedigree, invariably noticed first is the number of Champions recorded. The more dogs with Champion in front of their names, the more pleased we are and have great expectation that the pup we have chosen is well bred and will be a future Champion of its breed, producing more Champions under our own Kennel prefix. Regrettably, this is not always so.

The new dog owner seldom has any real information other than the names on the pedigree which provide only the direct line of ancestry and no other information. Consulting a pedigree is, therefore, of little use in a breeding programme unless one has been active in a breed for many years and seen the dogs named, knows their physical appearance and the quality of the progeny they have produced.

It is not difficult to produce a litter: mate a dog and bitch, and pups usually follow. If the union is completed without deep consideration and sound knowledge of the suitability of the mating pair, the result is often the arrival of yet another litter of mediocre specimens, some of whom, through diligent exhibiting, become very unworthy Champions.

If you decide to become a breeder of dogs, to be a quality breeder and possibly a judge of the breed, you have a lot of studying to do, since it is imperative for the health of any breed that you have a thorough knowledge and full understanding of the construction of the dog under its Breed Standard. The malady of breeders is the belief that all our ducklings are, in fact, swans, or will be by the time they reach adulthood. This is known as 'kennel blindness' and, if your aim is to be a breeder of sound quality animals, you must overcome this fading eyesight when assessing your stock.

Selecting a Brood Bitch

Having decided to enter into this world of dog breeding, the first decision must be whether it is best to start with an experienced adult brood bitch or with a puppy. It is far from easy to obtain an adult bitch of the quality you would require as a foundation of your line, and we would think it best to start with a young bitch. By this route, you are going to gain experience in raising and training her, will hopefully enter her for shows and, most important, you will have gained her complete trust and affection.

Take your time in finding your bitch. A breeder may tell you that both sire and dam of the bitch are Champions. That may be so but are they a suitable pair to have produced top-quality progeny? The union of two Champions is no guarantee of quality in their offspring. You may also be told by a breeder that a certain recurring fault has been eliminated in their line. Has it? Be cautious because

Ch. Rendorn No Retreat. A good bitch is an essential basis of good breeding.

Just the type of bitch who would make an ideal foundation.

this is telling you that there was, indeed, a recurring fault in their stock and there is no guarantee that it will not reappear in your pup at adulthood. However, keep in mind that no breeder can guarantee the quality of your pup at adulthood and often the quality will, to a degree, depend upon the manner you raise, feed, exercise and train your bitch.

Having decided on the bitch pup you will buy, the breeder will supply you with a pedigree which records the antecedents of the animal you have purchased. It is our opinion that the breeder should have researched the pedigree of both the sire and dam of your pup and, along with the official pedigree, give a back-up recording all the information possible on the faults and virtues of each and every dog and bitch recorded thereon. However, do keep in mind that, notwithstanding the advantage of advanced genetic knowledge, no one has as yet, as far as we know, bred a faultless animal of our or any other breed.

Finding a Stud Dog

Let us now consider your position. You have a good-quality young bitch who is, as far as one can tell, capable of producing a litter of healthy whelps. Hopefully, you will have absorbed enough knowledge of the breed to realize that great care and thought is needed before you can make a definite choice of the stud dog you plan to use over your bitch. By your study, the stud dog selected should complement the virtues of your bitch and strengthen the weaknesses you realize she exhibits. As well as the foregoing, the dog of your choice should be of sound and equable temperament. This is a most important consideration particularly in that over 80 per cent of puppies produced are sold as family pets rather than as prospective show dogs or breeding stock.

During the course of your search for the most suitable stud for your bitch, you will doubtless have approached the owners of several likely candidates. A good breeder and owner of a stud dog will supply you with a pedigree and be willing to discuss the suitability of the pair that are to be mated. Take your time. It is possible that the little-known Staffordshire Bull Terrier living at the end of your street might well be a better candidate for your bitch than the much touted and advertised 'Top Dog of the Year'. He may, most likely, also be more in line with your pocket.

166

As the breeder, you should by now have researched the physical and mental attributes of the stud dog and the stability of his pedigree, meaning that the generations from which he is descended are of similar type to himself. This is usually attained from what is referred to as family breeding, meaning that the stud's pedigree shows parents who share some common ancestry with your bitch, preferably in the first four generations, and are animals whose virtues have shown significant dominance in the progeny they have produced.

There are three recognized types of breeding:-

Outcross	The mating of two pure-bred animals who do not share ancestry in common.
Line-Breeding	The union of: Grandam to grandson Grandsire to granddaughter Cousin to cousin Aunt to nephew Uncle to niece Half-brother to sister
In-Breeding	Sire to daughter Dam to son Brother to sister

By observing the quite simple but very desirable family breeding, referred to as the 'tying together' of the antecendents of your bitch and the stud dog, you will at least be reasonably sure that the majority of pups at maturity will share similar virtues to those visible in the parents. In any event, you will have produced whelps who have what is called stability of strain and who should, at maturity, have the ability by virtue of the dominance of their qualities to reproduce animals of their own type and quality.

Inbreeding can reveal to the breeder the virtues of the line and the faults, enabling concentration on elimination of the faults and retention of the virtues through careful selection. An animal who is the product of a very closely related mating is, if a first-rate specimen, often capable of reproducing visible virtues in a large proportion of progeny, regardless of the breeding of the bitch over which he has been used. His characteristics are certain to be dominant in their genetic structure, and such an animal can be useful to any breeder with the desire to improve a physical aspect in which the progeny being produced seem to be consistently lacking.

Let us suppose you have been breeding to a carefully calculated plan for several generations and have progressed to the extent of strong, fine-quality puppies but, in spite of being of good quality, a large proportion lack one point. For example, you are producing what could be fairly assessed as 'flat sided' animals and know that a greater spring of rib would enhance the quality of your stock. If there is a closely bred stud dog available who has the ability to sire whelps showing a great improvement of this fault, it is well worth considering using him as a stud.

However, in the subsequent litter it is possible that other desirable points you have hoped to retain in full measure may possibly disappoint you, but you will have taken a positive step to improve the weakness in your breeding. If you then revert to the original family breeding programme you will usually find that in the next litter you have again produced the good aspects of your breeding and probably have improved or eliminated the weakness of the rib that you had.

The danger here is that any inbred animal might implant his unwanted characteristics as certainly as those that are desired. Therefore, always be sure you do not use an inbred stud with an inherent weakness. Study his forbears for strength and weakness before making the decision to use him over your bitch. You might be better off to line-breed which is, in fact, inbreeding but at a slower pace.

Looking back, there appears to have been many breeders who, for a few years, attain a seemingly almost infallible ability to produce first-rate stock, but then the dominance disappears. It seems that often they have refused to introduce new blood into their breeding programme in time to regenerate the vitality of their stock, which close breeding undoubtedly reduces, and perhaps some latent inherent weakness may have become dominant to such an extent that the quality of the stock has deteriorated rapidly.

Once you have decided on the dog to service your bitch, and the dog's owner has agreed to it, it is wise to ask him to have a sperm quality and count test from his stud. The result should be in the area of 125,000,000/ml. Therefore, if the bitch fails to conceive, the blame cannot then fall squarely upon the stud dog's inability to produce. If the union does not produce a litter, it is usual for a second service to be given to the same bitch by the same stud on her next heat, without further fee. It is wise, however, to have a written agreement on this.

Mating

Before the mating takes place, let us detail the dog's reproductive system. The dog is a placental mammal. This means that the bitch has a spongy vascular organ in circular, flattened form known as the placenta to which the foetus is attached, and is nourished and provided with oxygen by the umbilical cord. In parturition it is expelled and generally referred to as afterbirth.

Reproduction glands are known as gonads, in the female, ovaries, and in the male, testicles. Normally the male has two testes which hang between the hind legs in a skin sac known as the scrotum. The testicles produce sperm cells (spermatozoa) which unite with the eggs (ova) produced by the bitch in the fallopian tube; thus fertilization occurs. The male can eject millions of spermatozoa at one copulation. However, the number of the ensuing litter is determined by the bitch, depending upon the number of ova she produces to be fertilized.

In some males, one or both testicles fail to descend. When only one descends it is known as monorchidism and when both have failed to descend, cryptorchidism. It is doubtful that a dog is fertile if both testes remain buried in the abdomen. You need not be too concerned of infertility if only one teste has descended. We have known many good producing males who were monorchid.

No dog or bitch should be bred unless both are in the peak of their condition. In the USA many owners crate dogs. Crates are useful at dog shows where benching is rarely now provided and confinement of the dog in a crate is of short duration and more comfortable for the animal. However, continual confinement of dogs in crates is not prudent and, if the owner does not want a house dog, it would be far wiser to confine the animal in a suitable kennel run where he can move freely around. Downright boredom through crating as a daily routine may result in functional impotence in the male.

Do not confuse impotence with sterility. Impotence is the inability or lack of desire on the part of the male to perform the act of copulation. Sterility is the failure of either sex to produce sperm or ova capable, when united with those of the opposite sex, to

Bringarry Dangerman, the most important stud dog in the early history of the breed in the USA, had one testicle only partly descended. American judges faulted this.

produce living foetuses. In the male, sterility is easier to define by microscopic examination of the quality of the spermatozoa, hence, the wisdom of a sperm check and count on the male prior to a mating.

Long before the mating, do all you can to ensure your bitch is physically and mentally ready. Make sure she is not carrying unwanted weight, and ask your vet to give her a health check, also making sure the bitch is free from internal and external parasites.

If you are not sure of the receptive time of the bitch, you can have her tested. It is only when menstruation has subsided, normally

170

about ten days, that the bitch is in heat and usually will not permit copulation before then. From our personal experience and on the advice of most vets, the best time for breeding a bitch is between the years of three and six, by which time she will be fully mature and in the peak of her condition, will be strong and well able to carry, produce and care for her whelps. However, no matter what her age, she must be mentally and physically ready to take on this arduous task. If you want top-quality issue, you must make top-quality effort prior to the mating.

On the arrival of the bitch, leave the mating pair alone. Usually they will chase around, dog after bitch, which is natural and can be viewed as courtship. The bitch might be unwilling and snarl off the dog. This is not at all unusual behaviour, particularly if you have a maiden bitch or an untried and clumsy male. Give them plenty of time but if it becomes apparent that the bitch is unwilling to stand for the dog, you must give some assistance.

The owner of the bitch should, very gently, hold her head and support her under the loin, keeping her steady while the owner of the stud assists his dog by lifting the front legs onto the back of the bitch. Quite often it is necessary to guide his penis into her vulva, holding it there for a few minutes to achieve intromission. If the stud is a heavily built dog and the bitch smaller, she might need to be supported continuously.

The characteristic coitus in the male is made possible by the posterior portion of the penis (*corpus covenosum*) which is larger than the anterior portion. When grasped spasmodically by the bitch's muscles (*sphincter cunni*) in the vagina, it provides an injection of sperm into the bitch. The tie cannot be broken until the grasping muscles have receded; therefore, no effort should be made to separate the pair since this would injure one or both animals.

After copulation, an experienced stud will usually dismount and turn himself, still tied, so that the mating pair are in the correct tail to tail position. For the comfort of both animals, if the dog does not dismount and turn himself, or is having difficulty doing so, perhaps being the smaller animal, the owner must assist by carefully lifting the front legs off the bitch and placing them to one side of her. Then with great care, lift the hind leg in the same direction as the front legs over the back of the bitch, and thereby both will be in the correct tail to tail position.

You need not be concerned if they move around in this position unless the bitch is overly pulling away from the male. In this event, you must hold her and keep both dogs static. The stud cannot disengage himself until all grasping muscles have returned to normal size.

On disengagement of the mating pair, the stud owner should ensure his dog's sheath is returned to its correct place over the penis. If not, it can easily be accomplished by gentle manipulation.

It is normal for a second mating between the pair two days after the first.

At this point, let us discuss and put to rest the belief in and fear of telegony which is a previous sire's influence on the progeny produced by a subsequent sire from the same dam. We understand that earlier breeders believed there was at least an element of truth in this but, be assured, medically it is impossible.

No individual dog can have more than one sire. As an example, if you have had a double mating at a single heat, your bitch will produce a litter in which some whelps are by one sire and some by the other. A single pup arises only from the sire whose spermatozoon fertilized the ovum of the bitch; and sperm does not remain alive in the bitch from a previous heat-cycle mating. Issue from double mating cannot be registered with a Kennel Club by virtue of the inability to prove the sire of the individual offsprings.

Misalliance

During heat the bitch's instinct will compel her to seek out a male and, therefore, if you do not wish her to be served, especially perhaps by her mongrel friend living next door, you must keep her well confined. Rather than take the risk of becoming a breeder of quality mongrel pups, you might consider it wiser to board her in a reliable kennel for the duration of her heat cycle.

If such a misalliance has taken place, your Vet will administer diethylstibestrol. This should be given between the first five to ten days from inception which is the time it takes for the fertilized ovum to travel through the tubes to implantation of the developing blastocele. This often causes continuation of oestrus for an additional two to three weeks and, therefore, it is wise to have your bitch checked during this time to avoid the advent of pyometra which, although infrequent, may arise.

We firmly believe that should there be a misalliance, the pregnancy should be terminated. Through tremendous advances of veterinary medicine, dogs are now living for many more years than before and staying healthy, with the sad result that there are far more of them ending up in Humane Societies and Breed Rescue with fewer people adopting them. Regrettably, many of the misalliance results are handed over by the breeder to pet shops to sell with the excuse we have heard many times 'the pups have a right to life', with no consideration by the breeder of the quality of life to which they have the right. If, unknown to you, there has been a misalliance and, after due time you are sure that your bitch is in whelp, there is little you can do other than allow nature to take its course. The bitch will not care if her pups are pure-bred or mongrels and will be just as happy to have them and just as upset and disturbed if they are taken from her. If you decide to allow the bitch to carry and whelp, some pups can be removed immediately they are born, but you will have to retain one or two to satisfy the maternal instinct of your bitch and relieve her of the milk she will generate in the natural process of being prepared and able to feed the litter.

We have always found this situation rather sad, particularly for the bitch, and the blame for this happening must fall squarely on the owner who has not been diligent in keeping her safely confined during oestrus.

When not to Breed

Not all owners of bitches are interested in producing and raising a litter of pups. There are many who do so only through the belief that a bitch would be healthier, more mature or improve in temperament, or that it is just plain good for her. None of these is true. We have both bred bitches who have not matured any faster by breeding than a bitch who has not been bred and whose temperament has remained unchanged.

Breeding dogs is a hobby to strive to improve the quality of a particular breed. Uppermost in the mind of the breeder should be the knowledge that all progeny will not be to his entire satisfaction and that it is his responsibility to ensure that each and every pup produced finds a good loving home. Therefore, do not experiment in your quest for perfection of a strain, leaving a line of animals that might not be fortunate enough to have a good home.

It is a mistake to believe the old adage that a bitch should be bred on her second heat cycle. A bitch does not mature until three years of age and should not be burdened with pregnancy before her body strength can easily withstand the rigours of carrying, producing and raising a litter.

It is also a mistake for an owner to breed a bitch on the theory that it is natural for all bitches to want to produce offspring and that is the reason she will have the urge to mate with a male during oestrus. A bitch cannot reason that due to the mating she will probably produce whelps. After the mating, her instincts will sharpen to an awareness of the developing embryo she is carrying, but the instinct to produce was not the reason for her interest in the mating! It is purely a sex urge and not a desire for pregnancy.

Do not breed without sound knowledge of the pedigrees of both the bitch and chosen stud. Haphazard matings are the death of a breed. Do not accept the axiom that 'like begets like' and therefore breed without total knowledge of the antecedents recorded in the pedigree of both sire and dam.

No owner should breed his bitch without sufficient knowledge of the process of pregnancy, delivery of the litter and care for the bitch and her whelps. This is a situation of care–dependency between the breeder and bitch, a common relationship where the bitch is dependent upon the breeder for food and protection to enable her to care and raise her whelps. In other words, if you take care of your bitch she will take care of her whelps. It is, in fact, a partnership between owner and bitch. However, since the bitch is not raising her litter as nature would dictate in the wild, there is far more dependency by the bitch on the owner. Therefore, if you are not willing to participate totally in care–dependency, do not breed.

An owner who is obliged to be away from home on a daily basis and has to leave his animal alone, should not breed his bitch. Dogs are truly domesticated animals and, although they have strong instincts, through ownership by humans they are not totally competent to take care of themselves and their whelps.

If you own a stud dog, especially if he is of good quality, you are under no obligation to accept service by him to a bitch who, in your opinion, is not suitable or is carrying major faults. If you decline the use of your dog for this reason you are doing a service to your breed.

Too many breeders constantly discard their stock and buy more stock from other breeders instead of concentrating on learning the art of producing quality stock. A great many breeders, by virtue of numbers of litters produced, do become well known through their advertised prefix and, through this, eventually perhaps become judges of the breed, regardless of the possible lack of quality they have produced. Quality is far more important than quantity and, unless the owner learns and knows what constitutes a good dog, he should not breed or become a judge of the breed.

A breeder should always strive to improve the breed and not consider profit. In the UK, where the Staffordshire Bull Terrier appears to be the most popular terrier breed, there is a great demand for pups and, consequently, a well-bred and reared animal will command a price that only a few years ago would have seemed quite ludicrous. In such a free-market situation, any article for sale is worth exactly the amount the seller is able to obtain for it. Unfortunately, if the buyer does not know its true worth, he often spends far more money than he should and then is tempted to produce more litters, good or bad, purely for monetary gain. This also applies in the USA, although the numbers of this breed are small compared with the UK.

Both authors of this book have headed Staffordshire Bull Terrier Rescue for many years and have been more than disappointed, even dismayed at times, at the number of owners and breeders who give lip service to Breed Rescue but who rarely support with either money or action. Therefore, if you are going to be a good breeder, do not breed if you are not willing to be responsible for the progeny. Humane Societies and Breed Rescue will thank you.

7

Pregnancy and Whelping

Pregnancy

Your bitch is going to deliver a litter of pups that you have decided she should produce, it is then up to you to take care of her, encourage her and support her. Whatever happens to your bitch during her pregnancy will be your responsibility.

From a successful union of bitch and dog, embryos are forming in the uterus, a double-horned sausage-like organ whose walls are thick, resilient and internally corrugated, to which the embryo is attached and will remain for the gestation period. The embyro is contained in a membraneous sac immersed in amniotic fluid, designed by nature for protection from any blows the bitch may receive. From the umbilicus (later called the navel) of the yet unformed animal, a tube (umbilical cord) grows. The umbilical cord carries two arteries and a large vein which connect with the placenta. The placenta is the organ responsible for filtering food and oxygen to the new embryo, and through the placenta waste products in gaseous form are eliminated back into the bloodstream of the dam. Obviously, it is of paramount importance that you provide good nourishing food to your bitch, preferably three smaller meals per day rather than one large meal. Whatever you feed your bitch will in turn be fed to the embryo. Death of an embryo during its development might well be caused by lack of good nutrition.

External and internal parasites are definitely unwanted and your bitch must be kept free from them as they are easily transmitted to the whelps. As pregnancy progresses, the bitch will obviously be carrying the weight of the growing whelps and it is important she is not carrying excessive additional body weight. Exercise is thus important. However, do not overdo this but allow her to decide what is comfortable to her.

If your bitch is a house dog, do remember that you must expect her to have an accident or two through her inability to retain urine

Ch. Worden Queen. A lovely bitch whose whole appearance suggests she would be a good breeding bitch.

as well as she was able to prior to her becoming pregnant. Therefore, make sure she has access to an area she can use night and day.

The period of gestation is normally 63 days but it can vary either way. Pregnancy and whelping is the time you keep your bitch in touch with her vet, with frequent check-ups so that he will be cognizant of any deviation from the normal process throughout the pregnancy and whelping.

As the pregnancy advances it will not be unusual for your bitch to scratch and tear cushions and couches. Before you go into shock, remember that her instinct naturally impels this action in her desire to prepare a den for her oncoming offsprings. It might, therefore, be wise to introduce her to the whelping box early in the pregnancy. The diagram on page 178 shows the type of box we have

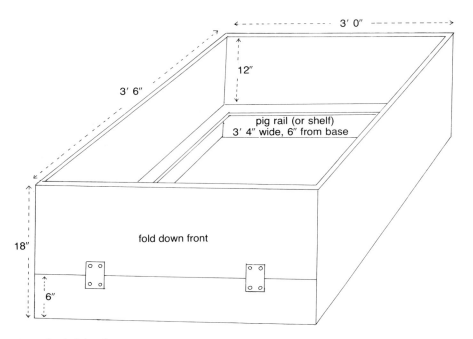

A good whelping box.

found very satisfactory and it is not difficult to make. It should be in an area that will give the bitch privacy but at the same time be where you can monitor her progress.

No two bitches are alike and it is not possible for us to recommend the type of bedding she will accept, if any at all. There is, however, one bedding you should avoid during parturition and that is a loose blanket. Unless securely fastened down, the whelps will be in danger of becoming enveloped in the blanket and you run the risk of their suffocating. It is easier and wiser not to put any soft loose padding and use strips of newspaper instead. Be sure the box is clean and, whatever cleanser you use, it must have no ingredients harmful to the whelps.

Nearing parturition, your bitch will become agitated, will probably search for privacy and a place to deliver her offspring, will refuse food and, when put in the whelping box, will tear and shred whatever bedding you are using. The normal temperature of a dog is 101.4 °F (38.5 °C) to 102 °F (38.9 °C) and it will drop several degrees when whelping is imminent. Normally the bitch will sleep soundly prior to the whelping to prepare herself for the arduous task she faces.

Whelping

You will soon see distinct labour signs of rhythmic straining to expel the whelp. First to arrive is a small water-filled sac about the size of a golf ball which is a buffer protection between the oncoming pups. The bitch will continue straining in her endeavour to expel the pup, which will usually arrive head first in his membraneous sac, along with the umbilical cord attached to the placenta (afterbirth). Your bitch will eat the placenta. It is known that the placenta stimulates the secretion of milk and should not be denied the bitch. It is one of nature's designs to provide a means for a wild canine to produce milk to feed her young at birth. Should the placenta or placentas be retained within the bitch, do not worry until all pups are delivered; then your vet will give her a shot of pituitrin that will expel them.

CC Sunrise Hustler (right) and Ch. Ashstock Red Buttons. Ch. Red Buttons was another bitch whose whole appearance suggests she would be good for breeding. She was the dam of Ch. Montbell Barborassa.

On arrival of the pup, the bitch will tear open the sac to release him. She will vigorously lick the pup both to dry him and induce breathing. Then she will sever the umbilical cord. If your bitch has poor dentition, such as uneven or undershot teeth, she will probably have some difficulty in severing the cord. If so, tightly tie a piece of surgical thread around the cord three to four inches (8 to 10cm) from the navel and cut the cord above it with sterilized scissors.

Your bitch will be very capable, even if it is her first litter, and will instinctively know what she is doing, so do not interfere in the delivery process unless she is obviously having problems expelling the whelps.

Pups do not usually arrive on a regular timetable. There can be quite long intervals between each delivery and it is not unusual for one pup immediately to follow another with a longer pause before the next one arrives. We have often thought that all the whelps have been delivered when, two hours later, another appears.

On the arrival of each pup, examine him thoroughly for abnormalities such as hair-lip and cleft palate. Pups with one of these problems will not be able to suckle. In the event that a pup does not appear to be breathing, it is possible that there is fluid in the lung. Hold the pup securely with both hands using two fingers to support the head, then, head-first, vigorously swing him in an arc from above your head to your knees (this is the procedure your vet performs when doing a Caesarean section to get the pups breathing). Do this several times. If the pup does not respond, rub his body with a towel, again with vigour, gently open his jaws and, with his tongue depressed by your finger, blow down his throat. Keep working at this and do not give up easily.

As each pup is delivered, put him to one side until all of them have arrived. They must be kept warm (80–85 °F/27–29 °C) by heat pads or preferably a heat lamp over the whelping box. If the dam appears to lack milk, the pups will need to be hand fed. However, constantly putting the whelps onto the dam's teats to suckle will often encourage milk secretion. The first milk for the pups is important in that it contains colostrum which immunizes against various viral diseases.

During parturition your bitch will probably be quite thirsty, so do offer her water; you can use milk with it. We have found that our whelping bitches enjoy being pampered a bit during their labour. Do remember that water must always be available to her.

Unfortunately, there might be a time your bitch will not be able to produce her litter naturally and a Caesarean section is required. You need not be overly concerned. In the hands of your veterinary surgeon it is not necessarily a hazardous operation providing you have kept your bitch in optimum condition.

I have been most fortunate to have had the opportunity to watch my vet perform a Caesarean section on one of my bitches. At first I was rather nervous and although not prone to fainting at the sight of blood, I was cognizant of the fact that this little creature needing help was, in fact, my bitch. I wondered if I could withstand watching this surgery. I knew she was in expert hands and soon found myself intensely involved with the procedure and marvelled at nature's design for the proliferation of a new generation and the skill of my vet. It was extraordinarily interesting and well worth watching. In future whelpings I felt more confident through the knowledge I had acquired and could more easily visualize and understand the process of parturition.

There may be other complications that arise, such as uterine contractions that are not strong enough to dislodge the foetuses; a contracted narrow pelvis preventing passing of the foetus, breech birth or other obstructions in the vagina. Obviously, all of these and other abnormalities need the expertise of your vet.

Care of the Dam and Whelps

Watch the whelps carefully, making sure they are thriving and that all are getting their share of food. Test the teats to ensure that each mammary is producing milk. If you find any lumps forming in the mammary glands, consult your vet. This can often be taken care of by hot and cold compresses on the mammaries. If the litter is small and the dam appears to have too much milk, you must relieve her by gently squeezing the teats to expel the milk. Pups use their front feet as a pump to obtain the milk from the dam's udders so make sure you keep their claws clipped to avoid discomfort to the bitch.

For the first few days after whelping, the bitch should be fed light and easily digested food four times a day. Fortunately, there are many good products available for specific feeding. The bitch needs nourishing food to avoid any deterioration in the amount and quality of the milk she needs to sustain her brood. If the pups are continually crying and lose condition and weight, obviously there

181

A healthy litter of pups at seven weeks. The breeder was Fred Clark.

is a problem and this is usually due to poor nourishment. At this point, your bitch is doing all the work and it is your job to support her and interfere as little as possible. She will feed and clean her pups herself. All you need to do at this stage is to feed her, make sure that the whelping box is always clean and examine the pups frequently for problems.

As soon as possible after birth, the dewclaws should be removed from the whelps. This is not done for cosmetic purposes: the dewclaws serve no purpose and can be a nuisance to the adult animal, and removal of them should be done within the first two days after birth. If left and then damaged when the dog is an adult, it requires surery which would be far more arduous than removing them at birth. We do not recommend that you remove the dewclaws from the pups yourself. When dealing with the dewclaws, your vet will also be able to examine your pups. It is a good idea to take the dam as well to prevent any anxiety at being separated from her whelps, and your vet can check her as well as the pups.

Should the dam fail to produce milk, the puppies will have to be

182

bottle or tube fed every four hours around the clock. Do not attempt tube feeding without having your vet teach you how to accomplish this correctly and safely. It is not difficult and, if the litter is large, it is easier and faster than bottle feeding. The amount of food will depend upon their ages and weight and, again, your vet will advise you.

If you are hand feeding, the dam may or may not be willing to clean the pups and, if not, you must take on this chore. After each feeding you will need to clean them by stimulation to expel urine and open the bowels. Using a soft damp piece of cloth, gently massage each pup's abdomen to expel urine and gently stroke or rub the rectum to open the bowels. You must be diligent and make sure all pups are relieved after each meal.

The dam's maternal antibodies can protect the whelps for up to twelve weeks. At various stages after this they will need distemper, hepatitis, leptospirosis, parainfluenza and parovirus shots. Make sure to take regular stool samples from the pups to be checked for worms. Worms can have serious harmful effects on pups if untreated and it is wiser to administer medication under the direction of the vet. He will probably require faecal examinations more than once since worms go through stages of development, and their eggs may not appear immediately in the first stool sample. It is important that you are diligent in keeping the whelps free from parasites.

Be conscientious in raising your whelps. It will take a great deal of your time and energy but do remember that the health and temperament of the adult dog arises from the quality of care and effort you, the breeder, are willing to give.

Should you allow visitors to view the pups? We think it depends upon the bitch. Some are very gregarious and will welcome a friend; others will try to hide the pups from visitors.

Pups are born blind and it is usually about ten days before they open their eyes. The will move around by pulling their bodies along by the front legs, dragging the rear legs behind them until eventually they are able to pull the back legs under the body into the correct position to enable them to stand on all four feet. However, it is not at all unusual for a pup to be unable to get onto his feet and usually it is the glutton of the litter.

It is easy to correct and does not harm the pup. Find someone to hold the pup, placing the back feet in the correct position directly under the hip. Cut a piece of adhesive tape slightly longer than the

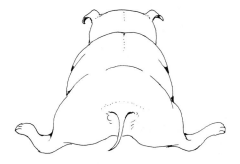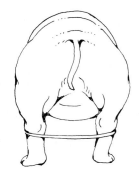

Taping a puppy's back legs.

width between the rear legs when held in the correct stance. Stick one end of the tape around one hock and the other end around the other hock. This will hold the back legs in the correct position and the pup will be obliged to pull the rear legs under the body when moving. After a few days you will find the pup moving correctly and you may remove the tape.

The pups will be ready to be weaned by three to four weeks of age. I have always found weaning the whelps to be hard work. Not only will they refuse your offerings, but the dam is likely to obstruct your effort. In my experience, the pups are never eager and helpful during the weaning process and I have found myself fighting off the dam, with the whelps ending up with food smothered over their bodies and none reaching their stomachs. To them nothing is as good as mother's milk and you might now discover how difficult and stubborn young pups can be. The dam is not going to be too thrilled either by what she will consider to be your interference.

So why not leave it to Mother Nature? The deciduous teeth of the pups erupt by the second to third week; the bitch will naturally be disinclined to allow them to suckle and will know it is time for weaning her brood. She will start the process of weaning by retaining her meals for a short time and then regurgitating partially digested mushy meals for her brood. Pups seem instinctively to recognize this as food and it takes little time for them to start lapping. Within a few days you will find the pups willing to eat the food you provide, and at this time the bitch should be put back on her normal pre-pregnancy diet.

To prevent the pups falling into the food container, it is a good

A litter of Silverlake pups bred by Lilian Rant. This litter included three future US Champions.

idea to use a saucer-like utensil, shallow enough to be easily reached by the whelps. Put it on a piece of wood just below the pup's head. By now they must have water constantly available to them.

If you find a pup that is difficult and disinclined to accept the food you offer, you may have to coax him by putting a spoonful of food under his nose until he licks, or smear food around his mouth. We have always felt that the change of texture from liquid to soft solid rather than the taste is one of the reasons pups are not enthused by the weaning process.

By now the pups will be spending a great deal of time out of the whelping box and, if the weather is good, they should be allowed to be in a confined area outside. The more exercise they have the more strength they will gain. Do be sure that you clean them at the end of the day, and thoroughly examine them for any little injuries through rough playing.

Naturally, the dam will be disinclined to clean her pups and they should now be able to defecate and urinate without stimulation. Even though the dam is not nursing her whelps and leaves them for longer periods of time, you will find that she is continuing to supervise her brood and has a great many things to teach them.

In one of my litters there was a very timid small male who was constantly being pushed around by his larger litter mates. I was beginning to get somewhat concerned and considered parting him from the litter when one morning I saw his dam concentrating on him, nipping at him relentlessly and roughly pushing him around. Suddenly, at the point I decided to interfere, the pup turned on his dam through, it seemed to me, his total frustration. She immediately stopped and, with tail wagging, groomed him from nose to tail and gave every indication that she was well satisfied with his performance. From that time he was accepted as one of the pack and held his own, and I did not again see him avoid a challenge by any other litter mate. From this I learned that the dam knew far more than I about raising her litter and, in the future, I continued to supervise the whelps but bowed to her superior ability and interfered as little as possible until it was time for me to socialize the pups.

The temperament of the adult dog stems to a great extent from the socializing of the animal when young and if your litter has been raised in a kennel-nursery environment, they must be exposed to house living. For a pup suddenly parted from his litter and dam, and thrust into the world of a new environment it will be extremely frightening and difficult for him. Therefore, give the pup time in the house before he leaves for his new home. In this way he will be used to people and children, and household noises such as the radio, vacuum cleaners, washing machines and other noisy equipment. You do not want a dog to dive for cover every time the telephone rings so do everything you possibly can to prepare the pup for his new life.

Do keep in touch and always be available to assist the new owners if they have problems. If they suddenly decide they do not want the pup, you must buy him back and find him a more suitable home. It is your responsibility to ensure that your pups have the best possible start in life. Naturally, it is nice to be known as a breeder of Champions but we prefer to be known as breeders of dogs sound in body and temperament who will contribute to the happiness and welfare of their owners.

8

Ailments and Diseases

It is our purpose in this chapter to give as much information as we are able so that conscientious owners will be better equipped to care for their pets. It must be emphasized that what we say should be used as a guide only, and any treatment we talk of is not in any way intended to be an alternative, but an aid, to treatment that only a veterinary practitioner is qualified and able to give. We do hope, however, that the chapter will give the average owner some guidance as to the correct action he can safely take that will be of help and benefit to the dog, without in any way giving an impression other than that it is absolutely essential to obtain veterinary advice as soon as possible.

The average dog owner will consult his vet at least once each year so that the annual booster shots may be given; at that time any vet will be happy to give the animal an examination, which will ensure that, superficially at least, your pet is fit and well. However, few animals are fortunate enough to live their entire lives without at some time contracting an illness, and it is the owner's reponsibility to be able to recognize immediately that his pet is not as well as he should be. A dog does not as a rule suddenly become very ill, unless of course he has been poisoned. Normally there is a period during which the dog may not be obviously ill but is also not in as good a condition as usual, and a good owner will quickly notice this. Some knowledge of dog care may well be of help and possibly even be instrumental in preventing the condition from deteriorating into a serious illness. However, we must emphasize that the know-it-all attitude of some owners can be, and sometimes is, very dangerous. Do bear in mind that unwisely applied, amateur first aid can do more harm than good and that only a veterinary practitioner has the in-depth knowledge and training to be able to diagnose accurately what is wrong and to prescribe correct medication.

There are, however, some conditions which can occur very suddenly and, although fortunately this is the exception rather than the rule, some previously learned knowledge can be of great use, even to the extent of saving the life of your pet. A case in point, and we have known several in Staffordshire Bull Terriers, is heat stroke coupled with soft palate. The heat causes the soft and excess throat membranes to swell, which prevents the animal from getting sufficient air into the lungs. Unless prompt action is taken the dog will very probably choke to death. We advise what action must be taken later in this chapter and we would point out that in a situation like this there is not time to wait for assistance: it is beholden to the dog's owner to know what to do and to be able to do it with whatever resources and materials are at hand. Very fortunately, it is seldom that a condition of this sort occurs, and most owners can and usually do see their dogs advance to a sedate old age without ever being forced into an emergency situation.

Veterinary science has, over the last few years, progressed at an ever-advancing speed to such an extent that treatment and cures are possible in cases which even a few years ago would have been accepted as beyond hope. This applies, of course, to general animal husbandry, not only to dogs, but as much is applicable to the canine as to any other branch of animal medicine. Nowadays our pets are able, if cared for properly, to live longer and more active and happy lives than at any previous time. It would be most unusual, however, for any dog, however well cared for and fed, to be lucky enough to reach an advanced age without some ailments, and the ability to be able to nurse and care for your pet efficiently when he is unwell is of great importance.

Obviously, it is impossible to explain to a dog that what you are doing will cure his illness and is for his own good but, if he trusts and has faith in you, as a well-loved dog will, he will bear and accept your probably unusual and unwelcome attentions with resigned equanimity. It is important to realize, too, that an animal who knows he has a secure place in the family and is well trained, will much more willingly submit to the administrations of the vet than would otherwise be the case. It should be borne in mind that some of our breed do seem to regard visits to the vet as often unpleasant and show great apprehension when they realize that they are going to the surgery, but it is seldom that a Stafford becomes so fractious as to be unmanageable.

A sick dog should be kept quiet, without any interference from any other pets you may have. He must be warm and as comfortable as possible. Conditions in his sick quarters should be conducive to him sleeping as much as he can. The bed must be large enough for him to be able to stretch out comfortably in. Restful sleep is of great benefit to a sick animal; it helps to conserve energy needed to combat more successfully whatever illness he has. Everything you can do that induces peace of mind in the patient should be done. As we say, he should be kept warm, but not too hot, so make sure the animal's sick quarters are kept to a moderate temperature either in winter or summer, and are well ventilated. If needed, keep a well-wrapped hot water-bottle in his bed. He must be kept clean and, assuming he is house-trained and is a naturally clean dog, it is sensible to allow him to go outside to relieve himself when he needs to. If he is too ill to be allowed out, do keep newspapers on the floor for him to use. A dog that is naturally clean will feel guilty and be unhappy if he has to do his business in the house and will need reassurances from you that, in the circumstances, his behaviour is excusable. If he is so ill that he is unable to leave his quarters even to relieve himself, he must be kept clean and dry. If this is the case, naturally the animal will be in the care of your vet and he will advise you as to the correct action for his welfare.

Do not over-fuss the patient. You must of course be sympathetic and supportive, but he will not want to be over-handled. Feed and water him as needed and allow him to relax and sleep as much as possible. By saying this, however, we do not intend to imply that the patient should be left to himself for hours on end; you must keep him under observation to be sure you are on hand to care for him if and when he needs your attention. Watch his general reactions carefully so that you are able to report accurately on any change in his general condition. The condition of his motions, sickness, or any signs of pain or discomfort should be carefully noted and reported to the vet.

Try not to let your pet realize you are worried about him. He will welcome and appreciate sympathy, but do not overdo it. That sick animals need rest and quiet cannot be stressed too much and good and sensible caring with a minimum of stress will help the animal recover strength and health much more quickly than would otherwise be the case. However good the veterinary care may be, good nursing is a very essential factor in aiding recovery. Veterinary knowledge increases every year and new drugs and medicines are constantly being developed, but home nursing of sick animals has changed very little if at all. Quiet, cleanliness, and common sense in caring for your pets are as essential now as they ever were.

STAFFORDSHIRE BULL TERRIERS

We have tried as far as is practically possible, to present the various ailments and diseases in alphabetical order but obviously, we will not be able to be absolutely accurate in this. For instance, 'Digestion' must be included under the heading 'Appetite', and so it would be of no use, if your query is with the dog's digestion, to look under the 'D' section of the chapter.

Anaemia

There should be very obvious indications that your dog may be anaemic. Usually there is a lack of correct pigmentation of the nose, lips and tongue, often coupled with a lessening of enthusiasm for exercise and play. Also, the animal's appetite may well not be as good as usual, with a consequent loss of condition. You should consult your vet as soon as possible for advice as to what treatment is required.

There are many types of anaemia that can affect dogs, and your vet may wish to analyse a blood sample to ascertain the type, in order to be able to prescribe correct treatment and medication. Often a course of vitamin supplements may be all that is needed, but do realize that this condition is always serious and, indeed, can sometimes be fatal, so obviously it is essential that you seek expert help and advice.

We have found that some Staffords, often those with a predominance of white in their markings, will take longer to develop the black nose and dark eye rims desirable in our breed, but are otherwise strong and healthy young animals. Usually time will correct this, but a course of an iron tonic or seaweed extract powder – obtainable from good pet stockists – will greatly speed the correction of this problem. In any event, this treatment could do no harm except that there may be some tendency for the animal to become slightly constipated, which presents no great problem except if it becomes persistent, in which case, you should consult your vet.

Arthritis

It is an unfortunate fact that arthritis is quite a common complaint in the canine world and, although the Stafford is no more susceptible than other breeds, it is a condition which should be watched for. It is usually extremely painful; the animal's movement deteriorates, usually to such an extent that he finds it quite impossible to exercise sufficiently.

Probably the most usual form is osteoarthritis, a degenerative and progressive deterioration of the affected joints, caused mainly by ageing. The correct articulation of any affected joint is impossible due to wear of the articular cartilage, which becomes badly pitted and is unable to prevent the joint from becoming badly worn and inefficient in movement.

The hip and stifle joints are the most usually affected and it is impossible for a dog with an arthritic hip or stifle joint to move soundly or without pain. He will be more noticeably lame after rest or sleep, easing slightly after movement has eased the joint, but he will invariably favour the affected limb, which will eventually cause muscular deterioration.

The condition is progressive and, though naturally more common in old dogs, it can occur at any age, particularly if the animal is hurt or receives a blow on or by one of the weight-bearing joints. Also, of course, it is found in animals with a congenital joint or bone weakness. Although most Staffords are considered to be normally a soundly constructed breed, we would again stress how essential it is to regard skeletal soundness and correct free movement to be of paramount importance in any breeding animal of either sex.

As far as treatment is concerned, veterinary advice is essential. Aspirin is probably the most widely used drug for pain relief, but it is a prop, not a remedy; your vet will be able, if he thinks it suitable, to give a course of injections which may well be of help. If the animal is overweight, he should be slimmed as much as is practical and his sleeping quarters must be kept dry and warm. A heat lamp will give comfort as will gentle massage of the affected joint. It is possible that your vet may advise an operation and this may be instrumental in checking the advance of this condition.

There are various other forms of arthritis which sometimes affect dogs, particularly septic arthritis, usually caused by a joint becoming infected because of accidental injury or possibly a fight. The joint becomes swollen and hot, and is so painful that the dog will usually avoid using the affected limb at all. Examination will probably reveal a degree of septicaemia, and your vet may have to drain pus from the joint cavity and give a course of antibiotic injections.

191

Bursitis is another type of arthritis, and fortunately for us it normally affects only the large and heavy breeds. We have never heard of a Stafford with bursitis but, for your information, it usually affects the elbow and surrounding area and, as with other types, is indicated by swelling of the joint. With rest and care, recovery of this is usually automatic.

An arthritic condition affecting the dog's vertebrae is known as spondylitis, and old dogs are sometimes affected. The lumber area of the spine is the usual site and it is normally both chronic and progressive. The animal will slowly lose all freedom of movement and give indications of pain. Treatment is as for other arthritic conditions for pain relief, and your vet should advise if there is no hope of improvement.

Appetite (Digestion)

The appetite of normal dogs will vary greatly. Some are greedy and, if given the opportunity, will always overeat and eventually become overweight. Others, though healthy, seem to be satisfied with very little, though they will still eat enough to maintain reasonable condition.

Some kinds of food are much more acceptable to an individual's taste than others, and obviously a dog will be inclined to ear far more of a diet that is very palatable to him than would otherwise be the case. Often owners are far too indulgent in catering for the particular taste of their pets and do sometimes create a finicky taste syndrome, invariably to the detriment of their pet's health. Care must be taken that the diet fed has a reasonably correct balance of vitamin and protein to maintain good health. If necessary. your vet will advise you on a suitable diet.

Occasionally a dog will develop what is known as a depraved appetite (usually because of some dietary deficiency), and will eat various noxious substances. Dirt, their own and other animals' faeces are the most usual. If your dog does at any time begin to develop this tendency, it would be sensible to review the diet and try to determine what the deficiency is. Animals who develop a tendency to eat filth acquire a habit that is very difficult to break and for a time constant supervision during exercise and vigorous discouragement is needed to cure this.

Burns and Scalds

If at any time you should have to deal with an animal that has been subjected accidentally to either a burn or scalding, obviously the extent of the burn is of the greatest importance. In the case of a minor burn or scald, apply a tannic acid dressing and subsequently, after a few hours, re-examine the wound and dress with a healing antiseptic ointment.

If it is a serious burn or scald, still apply a tannic acid dressing or, if this is not available, you can use a dressing with cold tea because of its tannic acid content. However, if the burn is serious, do get veterinary help as soon as you can. There is often serious shock, which can be at least as dangerous as the wound itself. Do be aware of this and, if required, treat for shock as well as for the wound.

Cleft Palates

This is an abnormality sometimes met with in our breed. Whether it is more common in Bull breeds than other types we do not know, and why it sometimes occurs is debatable, though there is probably some hereditary condition. However, it is also considered probable that dietary deficiencies and stress of the bitch during pregnancy may also be causes.

Cleft palate, often accompanied by a hare lip, are usually apparent at birth but, in any event, are always noticeable during the first few days. The whelp is unable to suckle properly, if at all, and will quickly die of starvation. If the condition is not severe, surgical correction is possible but would have to be done very soon after birth to give any chance of survival, and the pup would have to be very carefully nursed. Unless there is some very valid reason, your vet would probably advise that the affected pup should be painlessly put down.

Gastritis and Enteritis

These are often caused by overeating and by the intake of indigestible material. Often a growing pup, particularly when teething, will chew and swallow all kinds of rubbish. Wood, paper, rubber or practically anything available may be swallowed, causing a gastric condition. However, gastritis, particularly if acute, could be an indication that the animal has caught an infectious illness, although the possibility of catching the old common diseases such as distemper, hepatitis, etc. are usually completely eliminated nowadays by inoculation.

Indications of gastritis are obvious stomach pains, and sickness after food or drink. If not treated, it will cause loss of weight and condition. Fast the dog for a whole day, giving only cold boiled water to drink and possibly a dose of milk of magnesia. Usually this would be all that is needed but, if the condition persists, veterinary advice should be sought. For some days after an attack, care should be taken with diet. Fish, soft boiled eggs, milk puddings and other easily digestible foods should be the menu.

Enteritis is a condition of inflammation of the mucous membrane of the small intestine and is an isolated illness but is often used as a general term to include gastro-enteritis and colitis. The causes and condition are similar to those of gastritis and the same treatment is usually effective.

Hip Displasia

This is a progressive disease of the hip joint which does affect the larger and heavier breeds, but some Staffords are also affected. The disease is caused by malformation of the hip joint and it is generally accepted that there is a degree of hereditary probability. This makes selectivity of breeding stock of very great importance in eliminating any possibility of introducing this very serious disease into your stock. The acetabulum (a large cavity in the innominate bone of the hip) does not form a sympathetic correct joint with the head of the femur (thigh bone). The muscles and ligaments are unable to support the usage of the joint as they should, with the consequence that the femoral head tends to slip from the acetabulum with resultant lameness and great pain to the dog.

Unfortunately there is little evidence that a dog is affected in puppyhood. It is not until a dog is at least well into young adulthood that he gives any discernible signs that he is unable to move without pain, by which time, of course, he has hopefully become a well-loved member of his new family.

It is quite possible for vets to operate on an affected dog and completely replace the hip joint, but by far the best remedy is that breeders make certain that both the sire and dam used in a mating are completely sound animals. This is of the utmost importance for, as we have already pointed out, the trouble does not manifest itself until the animal is in the new home and it is obviously very unfair that, having bought a pup in good faith, new owners should be faced with the considerable expense of corrective surgery for a complaint that a really good breeder would probably have avoided.

Patella Dislocation (Slipping Patella)

It is true that small breeds are more likely to be affected by this, and there is no doubt that some Staffords are affected and an owner's recognition of this problem, followed by veterinary confirmation and correct treatment, will slow the progress of this complaint.

By and large the animal will move quite normally, but at any time is liable to start limping, sometimes to such an extent that he will not use the affected leg. Initially the dog will not give evidence of being in pain and will not resent examination. Sometimes the hock will rotate outwards because of the joint fault, giving the hind leg a pigeon-toed appearance, evidence that the patella has become displaced. A vet would be able to correct this by manipulation. However, the condition is progressive and the only permanent cure would be by surgery.

Parasites

Roundworms

Roundworm infection is usually associated with young pups and, if not treated, will affect both growth and condition. Affected pups are often pot-bellied and dull coated. They may well vomit worms and pass them in their motion. Your vet will prescribe the correct dosage for both the pups and the nursing dam.

Despite what proud breeders may tell you, there is seldom a litter of dogs of any breed that is free from roundworms, as the normal life cycle of these parasites is that they migrate from the dam into the puppy's foetus and usually reach the intestines within about a week of birth.

Quite apart from your vet's treatment, it is important to clean up

195

the motions of the dam right through the suckling period and even for a week or so after she has finished feeding her whelps. This is important not merely for the well-being of your own canine stock, but also because human beings can become affected by roundworm infestation, and your children could possibly become infected.

Tapeworms

This is the other most usual type of worm that dogs in the UK may well be infected with, but normally it is older dogs who have this complaint. Symptoms are again poor coat and general condition, often, but not always, accompanied by bad breath and general listlessness. This is, however, naturally governed by the degree of infestation, and many owners will notice and recognize the signs that their pet has a tapeworm before the clinical effects are more than barely noticeable. If you usually examine the motions of your pet, as most good owners do, and you notice small segments that look like small pieces of whitish-looking tape in the motion, report this to your vet; he will prescribe the appropriate medicine.

As far as we know, the normal method of contamination is by flea bite, so if your dog does contract fleas, do deflea him as soon as possible.

Fleas

As is well known, fleas are small, very active blood-sucking parasites who live and feed on the host animal. Several species may infest the dog, but the behaviour pattern is common to all. The flea spends most of its life on the host animal and lays eggs usually on the host, from whence they fall to the ground, where they hatch into larva, feeding on organic matter as available. When ready, the larva spins a cocoon and, about five days later, emerges as an adult flea. It immediately tries to find a suitable animal host on which to sustain itself and perpetuate its species.

If and when your dog has fleas, he will scratch in order to relieve the irritations caused by the flea bites. Unless checked, he may well make himself sore and uncomfortable, and lead to skin conditions such as dermatitis, that are difficult to cure.

Remember that although fleas live on your dog, their eggs infest every area the dog uses, therefore both the dog and his habitual venues must be treated. You will probably kill all the fleas on your pet, but they will return in a few days unless the whole area and all bedding are also treated. There are commercial anti-flea preparations on the market that are quite safe. Your local pet shop should be able to supply them, and they will quickly ease the animal's discomfort. Make sure you keep your animal free from fleas and, if there are sore scratch spots on his coat, treat with a soothing antiseptic ointment.

Rabies

This dreaded virus disease is, very fortunately, and largely due to our strict quarantine laws, so seldom able to affect the canine population in the UK that there have been very few occasions when there has been any reason for dog owners to worry or take any notice of it.

However, rabies is a world problem and does occur in America. Any warm-blooded animal can be infected and, once the rail link to the Continent is open, it is quite possible that infected animals could be transported or that animals, such as rats, could reach Britain much more easily. It may well become important that dog owners should be able to recognize and deal with this awful disease as quickly and efficiently as possible.

Rabies is usually transmitted by a bite, the virus-bearing saliva of the infected animal being passed directly into the bloodstream of the victim. It can be, and often is, transmitted some days before the infected animal shows any clinical signs of having the disease. The incubation period is normally from two weeks to two months, but in some cases is much longer, hence the six months' quarantine period being required by law in the United Kingdom.

The first sign of infection is a marked change in the behaviour pattern of the victim, though these changes – usually distress and loss of appetite – could easily also apply to the animal if he had a bad stomach upset, or had broken a tooth and injured his mouth. In these initial stages, the possibility of the dog having contracted rabies could easily be discounted. There is usually no great change in body temperature and a more reliable indication is that if a dog who is usually gregarious and anxious to be on good terms with his owners (as most Staffords are), tries to hide away and obviously wishes to be left alone, your suspicions should be aroused.

This preliminary period lasts for just a few days, after which the animal becomes vicious and will bite anybody or anything without provocation. This is far the most dangerous period and is followed by progressive paralysis; first the throat and masseta muscles are affected, with excessive salivation and absolute inability to swallow, and usually the lower jaw will drop. A great danger at this stage is that any examination of the mouth, often done with the bare hands, can result in contaminated saliva coming into contact with a wound or abrasion on the examiner's hands and would result in transmission of the disease, even though the animal does not try and probably is incapable of biting.

The aspect of rabies that attracts most publicity is the 'furious' or 'mad dog' syndrome and, though not all dogs go through this stage, those that do become extremely vicious and aggressive. The dog looks and is very alert, and will attack anything without reason or fear. Those affected in this way are extremely restless and will try to break from any confinement so determinedly that they will injure themselves in doing so. The condition is progressive, until convulsions and inability to control normal muscular reactions are followed by death.

We include this brief description as we do consider it very important that if our country should be cursed with an outbreak of this highly contagious disease, a dog owner should at least stand a chance of recognizing it and could take appropriate action. By far the most effective antidote would be general vaccination of all domestic animals, as is always practised in the USA, and a much more efficient control of all strays. Your own stock should be kept under control and in your sight when exercising. It is impossible to legislate for the complete irresponsibility of some dog owners, and the onus is on you to safeguard your own stock.

Shock

Often, when a dog has had an accident or even some other serious traumatic experience, such as anaesthesia or even a serious emotional upset which could induce a state of hysterical apprehension, a state of shock of varying degrees of seriousness could be induced. There is no known single reason for an animal to become shocked and there is no great need to be alarmed if it is a mild form. You will note that the pulse rate is faster than normal and the animal will be apathetic and cold, with a lower than normal blood pressure.

You must keep the dog warm and as rested as possible. Supply as much liquid as he will take. The treatment is really very similar to that for a human being. It is unfortunate that shock is usually a condition caused by some type of accident or trauma and, of course, this will have to be considered, but normally shock treatment would not interfere in any way with whatever measures you have to take to remedy the primary cause.

9
Famous Dogs of the Breed

The United Kingdom
(V.H. Pounds)

In Chapter 1 we dealt, to a certain extent, with how and why the line and families system was introduced to our breed and the reasons why it is now very little used by present-day breeders. Nowadays, breeding to any particular line would give little indication of the quality of whelps that would be produced, and most good breeders have reverted to what is known as family breeding, that is, using studs whose progeny is similar to, and related to, your own. Consequently, the lines of present-day stud dogs, even if traceable, are of little use to breeders.

Indeed, some lines – and I think particularly of the L, Game Lad line – I believe died out over twenty years ago. The last known representative was taken to South Africa in 1963, and Boylan, who kept a close check on this line (his own dog founded it), was quite sure that that was the last directly bred L line dog left. In any event, as far as breeding is concerned, the interest in the founding dogs is of no use to present-day breeders, although they are, of course, of great interest historically, and sensible breeders of today would be well advised to study any available photographs of these old dogs and to make comparisons of the marked differences between those animals and the winning specimens of today.

Although obviously of the same breed, the structure of the old dogs shows that there has been a profound change over the years. The first Staffordshire I had was a full 17in (43cm) high, weighed 39lb (18kg) fit, and looked every inch a real Stafford, as the photograph on page 116 shows. Breeders today apparently cannot breed a winning specimen 16in (42cm) high which weighs less than 42–43lb (19–20kg). Why? Judges, breeders or fashion? We have dealt with this subject more fully in Chapter 2.

In the photographs reproduced here, we have given the line the

200

An old photograph of Joe Dunn and Joe Mallen with Jim the Dandy,
the dog who was used as the basis for the first Standard.

dogs were produced from, but it should be borne in mind that the predominating lines, namely J and M, were very closely related on the bitch side of the pedigrees via a bitch known at the time of the first registrations as Silvers Queenie. We consider this bitch to be probably the most influential Staffordshire in the breed's history because, when mated to Fearless Joe, first of the J line, she produced a dog called Vindictive Monty, who in turn produced dogs who had a considerable influence on the breed.

Vindictive Monty's son produced some good show stock, but his most noticeable son, Spring Heeled Jack, produced, among others, two dogs who had a tremendous and lasting influence on the breed. These were The Great Bomber, owned by Joe Mallen and kept at his Old Crossguns pub in Cradeley Heath, and Boy Dan, owned by Bill Boylan and kept at his home in St Albans. Thus, two of the very best specimens of the immediate post-War period, when Staffords

201

A rare picture of Ch. Game Laddie with W.A. Boylan in 1938. Game Laddie was the second dog champion of the breed.

were in great demand, were available to breeders, one in the Midlands and one in the London area. Both were used extensively at stud and produced excellent stock, probably The Great Bomber the better of the two, though of course the predominance of good bitches was then, as now, in the Midlands rather than the South, and good bitches produce good dogs.

Let us, however, get back to Queenie. The founder of the M line, which was by 1948 definitely the pre-eminent line in numbers of registered progeny produced, was a dog called Brindle Mick, who was sired by Perrys Tiger ex a bitch named Brave Nell. This bitch was a daughter of the aforementioned Silvers Queenie, therefore the dam of the founding dog of the M line was also the dam of Vindictive Monty, whose get founded the most influential dogs of the J line.

By the late forties, these two lines, the most influential by far of

202

Ch. Madcap Mischief, one of only three pre-War bitch champions.

the six lines designated by Mr Beilby, were so related on the bitch side that by and large they could be safely mixed in any sensible breeding programme.

Let us now talk about the L line. Bill Boylan purchased Game Lad in Wolverhampton for the sum of £4 at some time in 1934, with no pedigree and no knowledge of his ancestry. He was a good, sound and typical Stafford. As we have mentioned earlier, he may quite possibly have been related to any of the early dogs of any line, except the B line (Western strain), who were located in a different geographical area – Preston – and were until 1935 by and large isolated from the main body of Stafford breeders. Mr Beilby believed that these showed some differences from the Birmingham dogs, chiefly in head properties, the muzzle being rather lighter than the Black Country dogs, though of course it is not possible to be dogmatic about any particular aspect of the Stafford, particularly in the early days.

The first dog I saw of this line was Eager Lad, owned by Mr S. Roebuck. He looked a nice dog to me, though I did consider my own dog a better specimen. At this time my opinions and knowledge of Staffords were essentially those of a novice, albeit one whose home had always housed one or two wire-haired terriers or Airedales, and I claimed to have some idea of correct conformation. It was the finer breed points I did not have the knowledge to appreciate. Eager Lad's son Tornado was such a lovely specimen, however, that even a raw novice could appreciate what a beautifully balanced, superb animal he was, and most certainly not weak in foreface. He was bred by Mr Harry Tomlinson, the then chairman of the SCSBT Society from his bitch Harandon Folly, a daughter of Ch. Midnight Gift, one of the breed's three pre-war Champion bitches. It may be of interest to note that this bitch was well over 17in (43cm) at the shoulder. I did see several of the Staffords she produced: all were at the top size of the Standard, which at the time read 15 to 18in, not as now.

It is not possible, at the present time, either to name or list the dogs and bitches who have attained championship status, with registrations running so high that Staffords are eligible to be awarded Challenge Certificates at all general Championship Shows, and most, if not all, the specialist breed clubs are allowed to hold a Championship Show annually. Indeed, the Southern Counties Society which is, after the Staffordshire BT Club, the most senior, has been privileged to hold a Championship Show every year since 1947 – well over forty consecutive Championship Shows, a record no other club can equal.

As with all other things in this world, competition varies from year to year, and this and many other factors have an influence on whether a dog of any breed attains championship status, so it would be very foolish to believe that a dog, because he has attained that rank, is a superb example of what a Stafford should be. Champions vary in quality as competition varies, and all one can say with a reasonable degree of certainty is that a Stafford who has been a Champion of the breed in the UK is invariably typical of its breed and usually physically sound. More than that one cannot say, and the Staffords I do mention are, in the main, some of those who have the priceless gift to a breeder of being able regularly to pass on at least some of their virtues to a high proportion of their progeny.

To illustate this, Eastaff Danom, who was temperamentally and physically one of the best dog Champions ever bred, was not merely that, but he had the genetic capability of reproducing his quality in quite a large percentage of his progeny. More important,

Brinstock Addition. Some years ahead of most of her contemporaries, and a certain champion but for the War.

however, at least in our opinion, is that he could always be relied on to give some of his virtues to nearly every bitch's progeny he was used on. Here I think particularly of rib. Very few, if any, of the animals he sired lacked a good rib-cage, both for spring and depth. When there is an animal in the breed who can be relied on to give any one physical attribute without in any way doing other than good generally, it can help enormously those breeders who recognize that the dog has this ability.

There have been, and still are, many Stafford Champions who are, quite frankly, what I would call a bit of luck. That is, an animal whose pedigree would give little if any indication of what the breeder could expect. Some of these animals have in themselves been superb specimens of the breed, but very few, if any, have this priceless gift of what I can only call genetic continuity, that is, dogs whose owners and breeders have put great effort and thought to the ancestry of the dogs produced, with the consequence that, as with Danom, he throws true to his own type.

205

Many other stud dogs had this ability, the first of whom obviously was Ch. Gentleman Jim, whelped in May 1937, and who, under the guidance of Joe Mallen, became the breed's first Champion. He sired two dog and one bitch Champions but, more importantly, his general standard was very high. During the time that most of his progeny could have been shown, the six war years intervened, when no shows were allowed, and, in the immeiate post-war years, Certificates were on offer at very few shows. Without doubt, had it not been for the war, Jim may well have been the breed's leading sire, both in the number of his get and the number of Champions made up from them.

His most famous son was a dark brindle dog called Wedneyland Kim, who in turn sired Wychbury Kimbo, who continued to produce good stock. Kim's other Champion sons, Wychbury Pied Wonder and Godfrey Pride's, were not such potent stud forces. The other dog who should be noted from Jim was Son O'Jim, who was a big winner but never became a Champion. He did, however, sire very good-quality stock, including Jolly Roger, who himself became a very potent sire, and among whose progeny could be numbered three Champions. Son O'Jim was a white pied brindle and his son Jolly Roger a brindle with white chest. Gentleman Jim's only Champion bitch was Ch. Eastbury Lass, from whom, via Colleen of Killyglen, came Ch. Linda of Killyglen, the dam of Eastaff Danom by a mating with Ch. Goldyns Leading Lad. The latter's breeder and owner, Mr Jack Altoft, continually bred very good-quality Staffords and was for years one of our most outstanding breeders.

Bill Boylan's pre-war champion Game Laddie was another significant sire: he produced three Champions, all bitches. One of these, Ch. Brinstock Sandy Bridget, was, in my opinion, one of the best bitches ever bred. Regrettably, however, although some good stock continued to come from this line, nothing outstanding was produced and the line gradually petered out. There is little doubt that it is now extinct.

Another notable stud dog of the fifties was Ch. Golden Boy of Essira, bred by Mrs Nancy Weller in the South. He was sired by Ch. Goldyns Leading Lad, as was Danom, from a home-bred bitch, Titian of Essira. When mated to Mr G. Down's Ch. Weycombe Cherry, the litter produced two bitch and one dog Champions. Both the bitches were owned by Mr A. Harkness in Scotland and were undoubtedly the foundation of his famous Senkrah Staffords, who from time to time still come out and win at the highest level.

Another significant dog was Ch. Wychbury Diamond King, who sired Ch. Major in Command of Wychbury, who in turn produced four bitch and one dog Champions and whose progeny still have considerable influence on the breed.

Another dog who should be mentioned among the galaxy of old-time stars is Ch. Head Lad of Villmar. He was, in many people's opinion, the best specimen of his era. Mr Beilby described him as being 'very close to the desired standard' and, indeed, he was one of the very best, a white and light brindle pied dog. His attributes were such that he would probably have been able to hold his position as a top-class specimen if he were being shown now. Unfortunately, his progeny never equalled his great virtue, and I think probably his best son was Milkern Guardsman, a good specimen, who sired one Champion, Gillcroft Guardson, over here and was then taken to New Zealand by his owner. Head Lad will, however, remain an important dog in the Stafford's history through a son, a dog which as far as I can remember I never saw, named Georgecroft Mandunas. Among his progeny was Ch. Bandits Brintiga, who was not merely a very fine Stafford himself, but when mated to a very good dark brindle bitch called Topcroft Tarbaby, threw two Champions, both very fine specimens indeed: Champions Topcroft Toreador (dog) and Topcroft Temptress (bitch). Both, particularly the dog, had a marked influence on the breed.

Sandra's Boy, a superb Stafford, was probably not used as much as he should have been. He was white, and there was, and to a certain extent still is, some prejudice regarding white Staffords. Joe Dunn once told me quite seriously that all white pups should be put down at birth. However that may be, Alf Tryhorn used him, and got from the mating Ch. Tawny of Dugard who was, in my opinion, probably the best Stafford bitch I ever saw. What a pity this fine dog had few opportunities to prove his worth.

Bellerophon Billy Boy, bred by Mr Alan Greenwood, apart from being a great winner, also produced first-rate stock. He produced five Champions, among whom a home-bred bitch, Ch. Judy of Brandenburg, was a really great Stafford bitch. Probably his best son was Ch. Son of Billy Boy, who in his turn maintained his sire's high standard and himself sired three Champions.

Ch. Rellim a Boy, bred by Mrs T. Miller, by Ch. Wychbury Red Riband ex Ch. Wychbury Middly Girl, was another very fine specimen, who sired, among other good stock, Ch. Rellim Ferryvale Victor, a great winner, who also produced excellent stock.

Ch. Subtle Difference, owned and bred by S. Warral. In the background is Ch. Corsair of Wyncole, owned by Miss Peebles.

Ch. Rellim A Boy, a very much admired champion.

A well-known dog who unfortunately never attained champion-ship status was Hydiamond King, who is assured of a niche in Stafford history, as among his produce was Ch. Game Flash, bred and owned by Mr A. Baxter, who in turn produced several Champions, one of whom was Ch. Rapparee Renegade, owned by Mr and Mrs Jim Bolton. The latter was the first of a continuous line of Rapparee dogs and bitches, some of whom – we think particularly of Ch. Rapparee Threapwood Handyman and Ch. Rapparee Rothersyke Vow – were used a great deal at stud and produced so many winning dogs and bitches that it would be true to say that a very high proportion of today's winning dogs and bitches will have Rapparee blood line in their pedigrees.

There are many other breeders who have, by the consistently high quality of the animals they have produced, from the very earliest days of the show history of the breed, done their best not merely to maintain but to improve the quality of the show Stafford. As the years go by, it seems that as one generation dies out and retires, another is already working to give continuity to maintain the standard.

Ch. Brinstock Glennagow, the last champion with the famous Brinstock prefix.

Ch. Hurricane of Judael, by Sheila's Little skipper, ex Crisp of Judael.

The first generation – Joe Mallen and Bill Boylan, Jack and Joe Dunn, Reuben Timmins and Gerald Dudley, with many of their contemporaries – are now gone. But before they had departed from the scene many others were continuing to uphold the breed's quality, such as the Hemstock family, the Lees, who continue with Nap Cairns' famous Constones dogs, A. Waters Ashstock and the Fensom's Pitbull prefixes, Malcolm Boam. Indeed, Malcolm Boam, in partnership with his old friend Brian Bates, brought out in 1976 a dog who was destined to play a significant part in the breed's history. This black brindle dog, Ch. Black Tusker, sired by Black King ex Lady Bella Madonna and bred in the north-east, was shown fearlessly, and I think was very seldom, if ever, out of the cards.

He won 14 CCs and was retired from the show ring at the early age of four years. It is very probable that he could have broken the record of 18 CCs won by Mr Ken Bailey's great Champion Benext Beau, but one record he holds is, in my opinion, of far greater importance. This is that he has to date sired sixteen champions, a record which, as far as we can ascertain, has never as yet been equalled by any other dog. We think Ch. Eastaff Danom with eleven is probably the nearest to this, and to make comparisons between the two would be unproductive and very foolish. Suffice it to say that both were great Champions and, by their stud prowess, will always command respect and admiration in the breed's history.

Moving into the 1980s, the progeny of Black Tusker are themselves having a marked influence on the breed. Other breeders

Ch. Fulfin Black Falcon, sired by Jununas Angry Axeman, ex Rendorn Black Bobbin.

211

Ch. Rendorn the Renegade of Linestaff, one of Norman and Mrs Berry's famous Staffords.

whose contributions are of great significance are Mr and Mrs Norman Berry, whose Rendom prefix has become synonymous with top-quality stock; Mr K. Brown has brought the Moekens prefix into prominence; Les Aspin, owner of the Scarthwait prefix, should really be classed as an all-rounder, both as breeder and judge, as he has bred various other terrier breeds successfully and is qualified to judge Terrier Group at Championship Show level. We do think, however, that his first and greatest love is the Stafford, and he has bred many very fine specimens. In producing Ch. Scarthwait Coachman, both sire and dam were bred and owned by Mr Aspin; the dog was completely home bred, a very unusual achievement. W. Watson also is a breeder who has been, over many years, a great asset to our breed, and this Scottish gentleman has for years consistently produced a stream of really beautiful quality bitches. If, in a catalogue, there is a Stafford with his Sanville prefix, I expect to see, whether or not it is a Champion (and it often is) a Stafford of the very highest quality.

The Lawlors, Fred and Rod Phillips, Tom Fletcher, Brian

Ch. Belnite Dark Huntsman, the first Staffordshire Bull Terrier to win the Best of Group at Crufts Dog Show 1989. The handler in the photograph is Margaret McElvogue and the judge is Mr Maurice Marchall.

Gratidge, Alf Tittle and the Pringles, together with other breeders of our best stock, such as Harry Latham and Derek Smart, have made and will continue to make great contributions to the breed's future. Even now they intermingle with the slightly newer generation. Bill McKnight of Northern Ireland has kept and bred Staffords for many years and has made his Belnite prefix a highly respected name. Indeed, a dog of his breeding did, in 1989, win the Terrier Group at Cruft's, the first time such a prestigious position has been attained by a Stafford at this world-famous show. His Ch. Belnite Dark Huntsman, has, by winning this, made sure that his Belnite prefix will be remembered as long as the breed lasts.

As far as we know, in the whole time our breed has been competing at Championship Shows in this country, that is since 1939, only one Stafford has been fortunate enough to win a Best in

213

Show award at an All Breed Championship Show. This was Ch. Wystaff Warfare, bred by the late Gwen Gallimore, and he won this honour at a Leicester Championship Show in the early 1970s. Warfare was a mid-brindle dog who excelled in type, balance, and soundness both of construction and movement, all qualities that appeal to an all-round judge.

We do hope, that after all the years of endeavour, the Stafford is becoming more acceptable to some of our all-round judges, and that they are becoming more appreciative and understanding of our breed. It should be realized, though, that only very occasionally has a Stafford won the Terrier Group at Championship Show level, and in Chapter 1 we consider why this is so when we are in competition with other terrier breeds.

Ch. Curfews White Orchid, owned and campaigned by first Fred Clark, and in the later stages of her career by Brian Barnes, was a superb specimen who, at three of the Southern Counties STB

Ch. Curfew's White Orchid at thirteen months old with her dam, Ch. Orchid Beauty, at the Manchester Championship Show, 1966. She won Reserve CC and Orchid Beauty won CC.

Society's Championship Shows, won the Tomlinson Memorial Trophy, awarded to the Best in show. No other Stafford has won this on more than one occasion. However, and in spite of being considered one of the finest Staffords shown, never did she win a first in group at an All Breed Championship Show, though several of her CCs were awarded by all-round judges.

To a certain extent, this situation will, in our opinion, continue, as the Stafford is physically in many respects not the average all-round terrier judge's idea of what a terrier should be. As the years go by, if the Stafford continues to be bred with much more regard for the Bull rather than the terrier characteristics, the chances of group wins must become more a hope than a probability. Photographs of the early winners such as Game Laddie and of our modern Champions will, we are sure, graphically illustrate this.

During the present decade many really first-class animals have been produced, and the popularity of the Stafford has increased at

Ch. Knight Templar, dog CC (left) and Ch. Orchid Beauty, bitch CC (right), Manchester Championship Show 1966.

215

Ch. Wallace the Wizard. An excellent modern Staffordshire Bull Terrier owned by Mr A. Hedges and Mr and Mrs D. Wood.

an amazing rate. Registrations at the present time are around an amazing 6,000 per annum, with a corresponding great increase in the entries at shows, particularly at championship level. Competition for Challenge Certificates is now extremely keen and we would consider that at the present time it is more difficult to make up champions than at any previous period in the breed's history.

From this point of view the great pressures of present-day competition must be good, but it should also be remembered that, with the popularity of the breed at an all-time peak, puppies are in great demand, and consequently command a high price. This

216

A red bitch who also exemplifies the very positive virtues of the present-day Staffordshire Bull Terrier.

naturally tends to attract a percentage of people who are neither enthusiasts nor interested in improving or even maintaining the quality of the breed, but only in how much money is to be made in as short a time as possible. These people will mate dogs and bitches without any regard for the suitability of the mating. If this type of haphazard breeding attains any large percentage of the Stafford population, many undesirable traits are certain to appear. Some of these, in such a powerful dog as the Stafford, will very quickly 'give the dog a bad name' in the minds of the general public, and the breed's present very high position would quickly disappear. We know that many people consider the breed is far too popular at present for its own good, and we are very much inclined to agree, but at the same time, no Stafford enthusiast would wish the breed to lose popularity for very much the wrong reasons.

One of the other unfortunate aspects of popularity is that there is bound to be a proportion of puppies sold whose owners are unable or unwilling to keep them. The breed's rescue services then

217

Ch. Scarthwaite Coachman (right) and Ch. Scarthwaite Temptress (left), two British-bred champions by British-bred stock on both sides of the pedigree. Their breeder was L. Aspin.

have to try to save or prolong the lives of the many unwanted Staffords, most of whom would be put down or abandoned. It is symptomatic of the times in which we live that most breeds now have need of the services of rescue organizations, but the Stafford, a strong-willed and highly intelligent dog, is possibly rather more difficult to own than some other less ebullient breeds, with the consequence that probably a higher percentage than most breeds have to be found new homes. It would be a wonderful achievement by the vast majority of responsible breeders if, in years to come, their vetting of potential customers was so thorough that these rescue societies could be disbanded. This would indeed be a red letter day in the breed's history.

This applies as much, if not more, to the owners of the stud dog as to the bitch owner and, although we realize that it is very nice to be paid a considerable sum to allow a dog to be used, it is the dog's owner who is beholden to ensure that, as far as possible, the owner of the bitch is going to be willing to take the responsibility of finding good, caring homes for the whelps produced. Otherwise, this problem of rescuing unwanted dogs may well eventually become so acute that the rescue organizations would have to begin to have many healthy dogs put down, a position which would, quite frankly, be such a complete reversal of the reasons for which these societies were originally formed that they could well be disbanded.

At present, there are seventeen specialist breed clubs in the UK, all of whom wholeheartedly support the rescue services, some of which are run by the clubs themselves. We know that these clubs do everything they possibly can to educate their members in the care of their Staffords, and give as much publicity and help to rescue as they can. The problem is getting worse rather than better and in the present climate of public opinion, influenced by all the

Akstaff Anchorman, owned by Mr P. Tottman who has for many years been one of the most caring breeders. (Bred by Miss P. McGlaghan.)

adverse publicity of the alarming increase in the incidents of dog fighting, all Bull-bred dogs are liable to be very unfairly criticized for even minor misdemeanours. Even now there is a tendency towards much the wrong type of person obtaining Staffords, which is unfortunate. However, the reverse and more optimistic view is that we do have, as aforementioned, many good breeders still producing many fine and typical Staffords, whose very desirable qualities as guard, nursemaid and friend will ensure the continuity of this wonderful, though at present rather abused, breed of dog.

The United States of America (Lilian Rant)

By virtue of the very short history of the Staffordshire Bull Terrier in the USA, we cannot compete with the many Champions recorded by The Kennel Club in England.

The first dog and bitch Champions of a breed are always remembered and, of course, for the sake of history they should be recorded first. Prior to the recognition of the breed by the American Kennel Club, we imported as much quality stock as possible to give us a solid basis. Two prospective owners decided they would like to buy a bitch of our breed and asked me to find a good one for them. I knew there was a good litter in Australia bred by Mr and Mrs Bruce and ordered a bitch pup to be sent to the USA. On arrival of the pup, those prospective owners had decided to go with another breed and did not take her. I was already over the number of dogs allowed to be kept in one household in the city and the bitch went to Judi Daniels. I have since often wondered if those prospective owners ever knew that the bitch pup they turned down became the first bitch Champion of the Breed Northwark Becky Sharp.

The first dog Champion was Tinkinswood Imperial. Like all dogs, he had structural faults but no one could fault his incredible intelligence and superb temperament. It was not unusual for breeders with pups for sale of the then unknown breed to call and ask if I would casually drop by with Fred, as he was called. Through this dog, nine times out of ten a sale was made and, if a male pup, it was invariably named Fred. He was, indeed, the anchor of the breed and died at the ripe old age of sixteen years. On his death I received many letters of regret and one was from a man I did not know who stated, 'your breed has lost its gentle giant'. There can

Ch. Logan's Jack Thrasher. A big winner in the USA who would have done well in the UK.

be no doubt that this dog played a very important part in the promotion of the breed in those early days and is probably remembered more for that than for being the first dog Champion.

I had imported a lovely Welsh-bred bitch, Prifddinas Petrina, whom I wanted to breed. She had produced a quality litter sired by Tinkinswood Imperial which included two worthy Champions, Silverlake Diablo and Silverlake Dreadnought. However, I felt she could do better and started to look for a stud who could maintain what she already had and at the same time give her what she did not have.

I was offered a proven stud from England and decided to import him to the USA. He was Bringarry Dangerman and must be remembered as an important and famous dog of our breed by the progeny he sired, even though he did not attain championship status. Again, I could not keep him myself and he became the pride

221

Ch. Silverlake Grenadier. His sire was Bringarry Dangerman and his dam Prifddinas Petrina.

and joy of Bill Daniels. Bred to Prifddinas Petrina, a litter of six worthy specimens arrived and were very much to my satisfaction. Three of the pups, especially a white bitch were, in my opinion, of good quality and candidates to compete in the show ring with some success but, for one reason or another, they were kept as pets. The remaining three were Silverlake Gemstock, Silverlake Gypsy Queen and Silverlake Grenadier.

Grenadier, owned by Lyn Lindsay, was shown in the Mid-west and became a worthy Champion and, equally important, sired Champions. Gemstock was owned by Jim Davenport and grew into a very good specimen and worthy Champion, earning Best of Breed awards, Best of Opposite Sex and Terrier Group placings under the handling of Erika Lorenzen.

On the recommendation of Jim Davenport, Mrs Barbara Elder came to see Gypsy Queen. This was a new breed for Mrs Elder and, naturally, she was very sceptical of my high opinion of the pup. With obvious reservation she took Mr Davenport's advice and bought Gypsy Queen. As is usual in our breed, the pup went through all the weird and wonderful changes of adolescence but it

222

Ch. Silverlake Gypsy Queen who became the first American-bred Staffordshire Bull Terrier to win Best of Breed at the Westminster Champion Show. Her sire was Bringarry Dangerman and her dam Prifddinas Petrina.

was very apparent to me that Gypsy was going to be a very worthy and outstanding adult specimen.

Mrs Elder had little interest in handling her bitch in the show ring and put Gypsy into the competent hands of Robert Jordan, member of the Professional Handlers Association at Malibu, California. He was not conversant with this new breed and was as sceptical about handling Gypsy as Mrs Elder had been about buying her. As I was the breeder of this pup, Mr Jordan did not immediately accept my

223

high opinion of her and reluctantly, it seemed, tried her out in a few shows. Those first few shows led Mr Jordan to campaign the bitch throughout the United States and wherever there was a Championship show, Gypsy was there. This was at a time when we badly needed country-wide exposure of our breed and if anyone provided that exposure, it surely had to be Mrs Elder.

Gypsy Queen was, indeed, a famous bitch of our breed. She earned 50 Best of Breed Awards, 18 Best of Opposite Sex and several Group placings. In 1977 she was the top winning Staffordshire Bull Terrier bitch and in 1978 crowned her career by earning Best of Breed at America's prestigious Westminster Kennel Club All-Breed Championship show held at the Madison Square Gardens in New York, the first bitch of our breed to attain that honour.

To our further satisfaction, the Best of Opposite Sex to Gypsy Queen was her half-brother Ch. Silverzend Satan, owned and shown by Jim Davenport. This was the first time we had a Best of Breed and Best of Oppostie Sex who were both American bred and both sired by Bringarry Dangerman. Satan was bred by Dana and Jenney Merritt from their bitch Ch. Constables Billy Club of Silverlake and Bringarry Dangerman. Billy Club was the daughter of the mating between Ch. Tinkinswood Imperial and Mexican Ch. UK-bred Margo of Rossile. Steve Stone and I were fortunate enough to bring this bitch into the USA from England and she was owned by Sue and Art Levin.

Satan's career was, to say the least, impressive: Top Staffordshire Bull Terrier All Systems in America 1975, 76, 77, 78; Top Staffordshire Bull Terrier American Bred 1975, 76, 77, 78; Top Staffordshire Bull Terrier Stud Dog in the USA   1979. Satan earned 67 Best of Breed honours, the last at the advanced age of nine years, and became the top stud dog, siring twenty Champions, as follows:

Ch. Davenhill Silverlake Dawn	Ch. Peck's Pimpernell of Stonefort
Ch. Starzend Waltzing Matilda	Ch. Logan's Chaos Thrasher
Ch. Starzend Moondust	Ch. Logan's Cock-o-the-walk
Ch. Davenhill Silverlake Lisa	Ch. Peck's Tuffy Luckey
Ch. Davenhill Silverlake Raven	Ch. Agincourt Annie Oakley
Ch. Starzend Satan Mistress	Ch. Logan's Molly Thrasher
Ch. Logan's Jack Thrasher	Ch. Kenmore's Angie of Davenhill
Ch. Starzend Wonder Witch	Ch. Starzend Ultra-Yonne CD
Ch. Trugrip Cotton Futures	Ch. Agincourt Belle Star
Ch. Martian Master	Ch. Agincourt Paladin

Ch. Silverzend Satan.

Bringarry Dangerman was, indeed, a famous dog and sired ten Champions from seven bitches. Other good producers were Brinsley Lad who sired four Champions from three bitches; Ch. Constables Billy Club of Silverlake produced five Champions; Ch. Cradbury Jonny Boy sired five Champions; Ch. Gamecock Collector's Item sired five Champions; Margot of Rossile produced six Champions; Ch. Reetuns Lord Jim sired six Champions; Ch. Millgarth Power Pack sired eleven Champions; Ch. Wystaff Warlock sired six Champions; Prifddinas Petrina produced five Champions; Ch. Northwark Becky Sharpe produced three Champions.

10

Living with Staffordshire Bull Terriers

(Lilian Rant)

Anyone can type but there is a big difference between the expert one-finger typist and a trained touch-typist and, in my opinion, there is a similar difference between a dog fighting and a fighting dog. If you want an obedience dog you train it for obedience. If you want a fighting dog you train it for fighting. I have never yet met a dog born with expertise for a certain activity.

Over the years I have talked to many Staffordshire Bull Terrier owners on this subject, particularly during the writing of this book. Without fail, the mere suggestion that the breed is by instinct or under any other natural conditions a fighting dog brings forth extraordinary reactions. I have found the most pleasant, polite and mildest of owners immediately become extremely defensive against what they deem to be a slur on this breed. It has, however, been my experience a great number of them alternate between being nervous that the dogs are going to fight and somewhat deflated when they do not. All dogs can fight but that does not mean they are a fighting breed.

I have been assured by the majority of my learned friends from the UK who have been my house guests in California, that if I continued to own more than two Staffordshire Bull Terriers without keeping them separated, particularly when I have left the house, I would have a gigantic battle on my hands. The warnings were given as friendly and expert advice, and while, obviously, it is always a possibility, as far as I am concerned, it will not be a probability.

The Staffordshire Bull Terrier has been my breed since the first one I acquired through a somewhat circuitous route during my wartime stint in the Women's Army when stationed in the dockyards of London. Like my co-author, I believed it to be a Bull

226

Living together in happiness.

Terrier. I had already come into possession of a Bull Terrier bitch, presumed to have lost her owners during the Blitz and who decided I would be a suitable substitute, with Army Life preferable to living by her wits. She was, indeed, one of the great dogs in my life, totally sharing the good and the bad of living through a war, full of fun, courageous and fanatically protective of me and her newly acquired Staffordshire Bull Terrier companion. They shared the rest of their long lives together in complete harmony.

I have constantly housed a minimum of four permanent Staffordshire Bull Terriers of both sexes, who over the years have had to share their home with various rescued dogs, primarily of my own breed, though they have included more than a few American Pitbull Terriers, a couple of delightful Bulldogs I wish I had kept, and many other dogs, of dubious ancestry and age, dumped on my doorstep. Additionally, for years the front patio was occupied by several generations of wild domestic cats and I spent two years raising a racoon from infancy to maturity, preparing it for and returning it to its natural environment.

I have always had an intense interest in animal behaviour and, as a member of our City Zoo and a trained Docent (unpaid guide) imparting basic zoology to school children, the opportunity to study wildlife was further opened to me. I also had the good fortune to live in an area surrounded by rugged hills occupied by a variety of wildlife including coyotes (members of the Canidae family) with the time to study them in their own habitat. I am always amazed and delighted that within the city and county of Los Angeles there are still large open areas rich in wildlife.

Coyotes in many ways are like smaller editions of wolves, the ancestor of the domestic dog, but are believed to be more adaptable and ingenious. My main interest was to observe the cause, effect and avoidance of aggression, competition and communication. I learned a great deal about aggression and competition but, other than the touching of noses in greeting, communication remained a

B. Barn's three bitches and one dog, who all lived together with little discord.

mystery to me. I constantly heard the calls, barks and yaps day and night, but failed to find a meaning or pattern to them. Often, particularly after dark, calls could be heard starting in the distance and continuing as a chain reaction involving up to a dozen calls over quite a large area, one after another. Whether these were calls for a gathering, with direction of when and where, I do not know because I am hopeless in following anything in the dark and usually end up totally disoriented and lost.

Coyotes appear to mate for life, stay as a pair, join a pack occasionally which seems to be of a social nature, but gather more often in rather smaller groups. The main drive appears to be of a competitive nature, understandable since they must survive alone or in groups, finding food, mates and giving protection to their young. Competition can, in turn, lead to aggression but it was apparent efforts were made to avoid aggression by postures that can readily be observed in domestic dogs who live together. There was social interplay by grooming, food sharing, resting or sleeping close together and, most important, submission to avoid confrontation.

The area that I was able to monitor was extensive, reaching almost into the centre of the city, which provided ready food from household garbage cans and which, perhaps, was conducive to more social acceptance within the groups than might otherwise have been the case if food was extremely scarce. Environment appeared to play an important part in their seemingly peaceful co-existence since in more confined areas there were occasional squabbles, often territorially induced. I did not witness outright confrontation individually or as a group. Since their calls could always be clearly heard in our home, it would have been easy to be aware of any serious confrontation. I concluded that the stimulus for aggression might conceivably be inadequate space as well as inadequate food supply.

Whatever I learned watching coyotes I applied as much as possible to the raising, keeping and understanding of my dogs. I allowed them free running in these hills; I always stayed in the same spot where I could watch them and where they could find me on their return. I knew that my male, Fred, with whom I was privileged to share the nearly sixteen years of his life, frequently mixed with coyotes and constantly with one male in particular. They apparently became friends when both were young and remained friends until they were too old to do much other than touch noses in greeting and sit side by side, doubtless in their own way remembering the past! As a domestic dog, I wondered just how much privilege he was given by his coyote acquaintances. Apparently it was quite extensive in that I noted a den where I knew were coyote whelps and was surprised to see Fred emerging from it at a most unconcerned slow trot, followed by the dam at an equally unconcerned slow trot faking a rear-end attack with obvious lack of animosity, enthusiasm and intent.

I was impressed by the adults' tolerance for the young, and the social experiences of the very young seem to influence their behaviour as adults, which I found with my own bitches in their ability in rearing their offsprings. The younger bitches, when allowed interaction and free access with older experienced bitches with whelps, have been more efficient and caring for their young. Males, if allowed this interaction, seem also more tolerant. On this theory I have, over many years and litters, allowed free access to the nursery at all times with no problems.

The nursery building was by the side of the house where my whelping bitches could be given total privacy if they wished. It has been my experience that the bitches would, at times, growl off canine visitors, and they left showing no animosity or ruffled feathers, apparently understanding the wish of the bitch. If welcomed by the dam, it was not unusual for my dogs, individually or together, to spend time in the nursery, staying as long as allowed by her.

As litters began to grow and become active the dam still had control but it was quite apparent that other dogs, of both sexes, were welcomed to assist in the raising of the pups. At one time I had two bitches in whelp, three weeks apart. They had separate nursery quarters and produced between them thirteen pups. There was at the same time co-operation from my male and third bitch and no problems with the two dams. As soon as all the pups were strong enough to romp around, the two litters constantly mixed together. It was, as usual, a peaceful pack joint effort until the pups were ten to twelve weeks of age and left home to start their own lives. I personally do not like to send pups out into their new world before ten weeks, by which time they should be strong, partially, if not completely, housebroken and, for their age, socially adjusted animals. Neither do I believe in curtailing the length of time the bitch wishes to continue feeding them herself, including weaning by regurgitating her own food.

I discovered this co-existence of co-operation and non-aggression to be the same with a bitch and her whelps who were not my own. A very good friend had the need to have someone house her bitch and whelps for several days and brought them to me. The whelps were quite young. Following the theory of open nursery, the bitch, pups and my dogs settled in total harmony with the same interaction between them. This, however, might have been largely due to the owner of the bitch keeping her three Staffordshire Bull Terriers in a like environment, and perhaps there was trust and non-aggression since the adults knew each other.

Acceptance of animals of the same family (Canidae) is one thing, but with the arrival of Mr Mac, an orphaned five-week-old racoon, I wondered if I could maintain peaceful co-existence, particularly in that he would need to be integrated with my dogs and it would be two years before he would be sexually mature and able to return to his natural environment. I was also very concerned that I did not have previous experience or sufficient knowledge of this species to teach him the skills he would need for his survival in his own environment. What I did know was they are fun-loving mischievous creatures, extraordinarily courageous and, when necessary, capably aggressive as witnessed by the damage sustained by my male after a confrontation with an adult male racoon. The introduction with my bitches was normal and with no problems, but not so with Fred. It was obvious that he regarded this little creature as an enemy, doubtless recalling the confrontations he endured.

Mr Mac had to be bottle fed so I started by insisting Fred sat with me during feeding, allowing him to smell and investigate the newcomer. Gradually, the tense and belligerent attitude changed and from then on they were the greatest of friends. I had a litter of pups the same age as Mr Mac and he joined them in all their games, and was accepted by the dam and all my dogs. A year later, one of the bitch pups from the litter came back to me and I was totally surprised, and delighted, that she and Mac instantly greeted each other with great enthusiasm.

Mac grew up with the distinct advantage of having Fred's protection from other male racoons on whose territory Mr Mac appeared to be living, albeit our own backyard. It was a wonderful two years' experience. He eventually went off to live his own life as Nature intended he should, armed with a few additional skills learned from my Staffordshire Bull Terriers to aid in his survival.

He was greatly missed for a very long time but he was a creature of the wild and not a domestic animal, deserving of his own life experience.

My present pack of four – two males and two females – are just as co-operative and no different in temperament and ability from all my previous dogs, even though my now eleven-year-old male did not join our pack until he was over five years of age with a reputation of being able to take care of himself.

During the writing of this book, we are living in a farmhouse surrounded by pastures of cattle and sheep. My dogs were separated from me for UK quarantine which they endured and survived with the usual Staffordshire Bull Terrier good humour and *joie de vivre*. However, on arrival here, within a very short time I realized that to them the sight of the sheep conjured up visions of lamb chops for dinner! For peaceful existence, coupled with the desire to remain in the house until this book could be finished, a solution had to be found. This was particularly so when I was advised that farmers, under the law, are permitted to shoot on sight any dog thought to be worrying sheep. The solution came in a most delightful way in the form of three orphan lambs needing a substitute mother. The chaos, difficulties and frustrations endured by my dogs in their effort to raise three lambs in a similar manner to Staffordshire Bull Terrier pups are too long to include in this book. Suffice to say, the lambs survived their efforts and are now adult sheep, and the dogs have long since given up thoughts of lamb chops.

Over the years, with generations of Staffordshire Bull Terriers, particularly as I seem incapable of being happy with just owning one dog, I have found ways, by studying the coyote family, of reducing aggression, or rather channelling it in the right direction by understanding the needs of the dog as a dog.

To satisfy the need for competition, I use the simple device most owners use – throwing a ball. No one dog is left out. If one is less able to compete fully than the others, I give that dog a chance by making sure the ball is often aimed in his direction. The dog then feels fully involved and competing; in this way, his competitive instinct is being satisfied. They always eat in close proximity to each other and, although I am careful to avoid overeating by one at the expense of another, they are allowed to approach each others' food dish to clean up any particles left behind. All are given a bone, and those not buried for resurrection as a tasty morsel when ripe

Dorelu Red Sam. Dogs must be kept fit and happy.

enough to be enjoyed on the best armchair are interchanged between them; this constantly provides a basis for food sharing. If only one bone survives, it is not at all unusual for one dog to be enjoying it and the others snoozing and waiting with great patience for their turn. I found this peaceful procedure of bone sharing to be the one most unnerving experience for my house guests!

At some time during the day – and I am quite rigid on this behaviour – after exercise when the dogs are resting, I join them on the floor to be at their level where they then gather around in close contact and I am usually subjected to a great deal of grooming. I have, in fact, the cleanest ears in town! This is our social sharing time which reinforces submission and lack of aggression toward each other and to me as the pack leader. I am their pack leader and friend and they live without fear of physical punishment which I have never found the need to administer.

When I was totally confident of my rescued lodgers, they too enjoyed our daily outings and joined the pack routine. I might add here that other Staffordshire Bull Terrier breeders and owners with their dogs have frequently joined us in the hills and there have often been around ten dogs. Occasionally there was a squabble, but we seldom interfered since it was all noise and no substance. I have not always lived in an area with easy access for exercise. In fact, I kept my Staffordshire Bull Terriers in a top-floor flat in London and still maintained a peaceful co-existence.

Man is considered to be the most aggressive species in the animal world and, from that viewpoint, I believe he often uses that aggression as a tool for the training and control of his dogs. Aggression appears to be the product of the environment within which the dog must live and, since that environment is dictated by the owner, it must be believed that aggression is induced or reduced by the owner. It is so very easy to teach aggression to young animals and, therefore, produce aggressive adults. The dog adopts and reflects the pattern of behaviour required by his environment and upbringing, suggesting to me that there is little substance to the steadfast belief that the Staffordshire Bull Terrier has only one unsurmountable instinct, that of a fighting dog, unable to co-exist peacefully with any other animal.

The principal instinct of man and animals is the same – survival. If confronted with a situation of having to fight to survive, both will fight. Therefore, a dog who through his owner's training and encouragement, is placed in the position of having no alternative other than to defend himself, will fight to survive. The prime instinct is not to fight but to survive, and it is then a dog fighting and not a fighting dog.

If this myth of a fighting dog is accepted, the dog cannot then project the true character and wonderful temperament he has to offer and, in my opinion, the owner is the loser, never to enjoy or experience the wonderful and rewarding life I have had, and will continue to have, with my Staffordshire Bull Terriers.

Useful Addresses

Staffordshire Bull Terrier Clubs

Alyn and Deeside
Mrs M. Byrne
20 Beeston Road
Higher Kinnerton
Clwyd
Tel. 0224 660758

East Anglian
Mrs J. Shorrock
Weston Hall
Beccles
Tel. 0502 713472

East Midlands
Mr J. Monks
88 Briars Meads
Oadby
Leicester LE2 5WD
Tel. 0533 713122

Merseyside
Mr R. Hudson
38 Gourley Road
Liverpool L13 4AY
Tel. 051 259 3811

Morecambe & Cumbria
Mrs C. Sumner
10 Windermere Avenue
Farington
Leyland
Lancashire
Tel. 0772 436203

North Eastern
Mr G. Purvis
1 Lyons Cottages
Hetton-Le-Hole
Tyne & Wear DH5 0HU
Tel. 091 526 7817

Northern Counties
Mr I. Keyes
44 Glanford Road
Brigg
South Humberside DN20 8DJ
Tel. 0652 55535

Northern Ireland
Mr. W. McKnight
9 Mountcolle Gardens
Belfast
Tel. 0232 711608

North of Scotland
Mrs K. Carmichael
97 Malcolm Road
Peterculter
Aberdeen
Tel. 0224 734441

North West
Mrs C. Atherton
Cross Cottage
Shaw Brow
Whittle-Le-Woods
Chorley
Lancashire
Tel. 02572 60273

Notts & Derby
Mr B. Grattidge
3 Angela Avenue
Kirkby-in-Ashfield
Nottinghamshire
Tel. 0623 752340

Potteries
Mr Steve Leyland
333, Bermersley Road
Ridgeway
Stoke on Trent
Staffordshire

Scottish
Mr A. Harkness
Senkrah Villa
Chapel Street
Carluke
Lanarkshire
Tel. 0555 70564

The Staffordshire Bull Terrier Club
Mr J. Beaufoy
Wyefare Cottage
Yew Tree Lane
Bewdley
Worcestershire DY12 2PJ
Tel. 0299 40382

Southern Counties
Mrs I. Baker
41 Vernham Road
London SE18 3EY
Tel. 081 854 8482

South Wales
Mr J. Holle
22 Heol-Y-Gors
Townhill
Swansea
Tel. 0792 582597

Western
Mrs M. Broadstock
11 Greenfield Terrace
Abercynon
Mid. Glamorgan CF45 4TL
Tel. 0443 742009

Addresses of Staffordshire Bull Terrier Clubs in the USA are obtainable from the Staffordshire Bull Terrier Club of America:

Steve Eltinge
President
725 Croft Lane
Solvang
California 93463
USA

Bibliography

Beilby, H.N. *The Staffordshire Bull Terrier* Blackie & Son Ltd. (1948)

Croxton Smith, A. *About our Dogs* Ward Lock & Co. Ltd. (1931)

Los Angeles Zoo Library Docent Lectures in the family Canidae (1960)

McDowell Lyon *The Dog in Action* Howell Book House Inc. (1978)

Miller *Anatomy of the Dog* Evans & Christensen (1970)

National Geographic Book of Dogs *Man's Best Friend* The National Geographic Society (1966)

Onstott, Philip *The New Art of Breeding Better Dogs* (1968)

Smythe, R.H. *The Dog, Structure and Movement* W. Foulsham & Co. Ltd. (1948)

Sporting Magazine, Vols. 2 to 10 J. Wheble & J. Pitman (1818–22)

The Stafford Magazine (Southern Counties Staffordshire Bull Terrier Society, UK)

Witney, Leon F. *The Complete Book of Dog Care* Howell Book House Inc. (1937)

Index

adolescence, 137–8
American Kennel Club, 26
  registration, 131–2
anaemia, 190
appetite, 192
arthritis, 190
Aspin, L., 212

Baily, K., 211
Bandits Belle Lettres, 20
Beilby, H.N., 15, 36, 202–3
Bellerephon Billy Boy, Ch., 207
benching, 148–9
Benext Beau, Ch., 211
Berry, N., 212
Black Tusker, Ch., 211
Boam, M., 210
Bolton, J., 209
Boylan, W.A., 36, 200–1
Breed Standard, American, 43–5
  discussion of, 47–113
  in judging, 159–62
  new, 111–12
  UK, 41–3
breeding, 163–175
Bringarry Dangerman, 221
brood bitch, 164
  care of, 176–83
  selecting a, 164–6
Bull Terrier, 27
burns, 193

Cairns, A.W.A., 34
calories, 142
classes, 155–7

cleft palates, 193
coat colour, 98–100
  genetics of, 99–100
Curfews White Orchid, Ch., 214

dam, care of, see brood bitch
Daniels, W., 20, 222
  Mrs J., 220
Davenport, J., 222–4
dentition, 59–63
dewclaws, 92, 182

Eltinge, S., 19
ears, 57
Eastaff Danom, Ch., 204
Elder, B., 222, 223, 224
enteritis, 193
exercise, 144

famous dogs, UK, 200–20
  USA, 220–5
feeding, hand, 183
feet, 92
Firestreak Red Rover, 20
Fitz Barnard, 29
fleas, 196–7
Forrester, Mrs M., 17

Gallimore, Mrs G., 214
Game Lad, 15
Game Laddie, Ch., 15
gastritis, 193
Gentleman Jim, Ch., 206
gestation, 177
Golden Boy Of Essira, Ch., 206

Goldwyns Leading Lad, Ch., 206
Gordon, J., 16–8, 33, 47

Harkness, A., 206
head, 47
Head Lad Of Villmar, Ch., 207
height, 94
heat stroke, 188
hip displasia, 194

Idston, 31
impotence, 169
in-breeding, 167–8

J line, 201
Jolly Roger, 206
judging, 157
    method, 158

L line, 200
line-breeding, 167–8

M line, 201
Mallen, J., 206
mating, 169–72
    double, 172
    misalliance, 172–3
McKnight, W., 213
movement, 100–2, 104–6. 161–2
Meyrick, 30

nutrition, 141–4

obesity, 142
outcross, 167

patella, 195
pedigree, 129
Pitbull Terrier, 26–7, 54, 66
presentation, 147
puppy, 123–7, 134–7
    choosing a, 121–9
    diet of, 134
    registration of, 129
    training, 135–7

see also whelps
purpose of breed, 26

rabies, 197
Rant, Larry, 20–4
registration, 26, 145
Rellim A Boy, Ch., 207
rescue, 175, 217–19
Ring Steward, 152
    training, 147
Rosenfield, Mrs, 20

Sandras Boy, Ch., 207
SBT Clubs, 150, 235
    Finnish, 16
    USA, 18
Savage, C.L., 24
shock, 198–9
showing, 145
show, Uk, 148–50
    presentation, 153
    USA, 150–5
Silverlake Gypsy Queen, Ch., 222,
    223, 224
Silverzend Satan, Ch., 224
Silvers Queenie, 201–2
Smith, C., 17
social behaviour, 232–3
soundness, 109–11
sperm testing, 168
Stone, S., 16–17, 24
stud dog, 166–72

Tawney of Dugard, Ch., 207
Thomlinson, H., 204
Tinkinswood Imperial, Ch., 18, 22,
    220
Tinkler, K., 20
Tittle, A., 15–16
Tornado, 204
training, 135–41

Watson, W., 212
weaning, 184
weight, 94

Widneyland Kim, Ch., 206
Williams, Claud, 20
whelping, 179–181
whelps, 181–6

hand feeding, 182–3
worms, 195–6
Wychbury Diamond King, Ch., 207
Wystaff Warfare, Ch., 214